Chalk and Lime Gardening

Gardening

°A GUIDE TO SUCCESS ON ALKALINE SOILS

Sarah Coles

THE
CROWOOD PRESS

First published in 2005 by
The Crowood Press Ltd
Ramsbury, Marlborough
Wiltshire SN8 2HR

www.crowood.com

British Library Cataloguing-in-Publication Data

A catalogue record for this book is available from the British Library.

ISBN 1 86126 738 X

Typeface used: M Plantin.

Typeset and designed by
D & N Publishing
Lambourn Woodlands, Hungerford, Berkshire.

Printed and bound in Malaysia by Times Offset (M) Sdn. Bhd.

Contents

Acknowledgements

So many people have helped me, with knowledge and expertise, hospitality and sustenance, as well as letting me photograph their gardens and much more. I must thank Ken Muir, of Ken Muir Soft Fruits, Judith McAweaney and Thompson & Morgan, who supplied seeds and potatoes for trialling, Nick Randall of West Meters Ltd, for supplying soil-testing apparatus, Terence Baker, of the Botanic Nursery, Phillip Nelson, Head Gardener of Parcevall Hall Gardens, Tom Palmer, of Leckford Fruit Farms, Mike Buffin, former Curator of the Sir Harold Hillier Gardens for checking the nomenclature – though any remaining slips are mine – all the honorary county organizers of the National Gardens Scheme who wrote and telephoned about alkaline gardens in their vicinity, and my husband Bob Coles, Humphrey and Josephine Boyle, Nicholas and Henrietta Wood, Victoria Wakefield, Dick and Gillian Pugh, Marion Wake, Ewan and Jenny Harper, David and Anne Hanson, Michael and Diane Schultz, Elizabeth Wheeler, Gillian Mylne, Sally Curtis, David Freeman, Jonquil Hinds, Douglas and Margaret Fuller, Michael and Margaret Highton, Martin and Rosie Lowry, Richard and Sue Young, Richard Pim, Mike and Ann Jarman, Roger and Margaret Pearson, Andrew Conduct, James and Diana Ekins, Adrian and Molly Smith and, especially, my thanks to Nicholas and Jo Tatton Brown for years of garden help, visiting and advice.

OPPOSITE PAGE: Actinidia kolomikta *'Tricolor', with leaves' white, pink and green.*

RIGHT: *Natural limestone at Parcevall Hall, Yorkshire, planted with ferns,* Sedum *and* Daphne tangutica.

Introduction

Mark those rounded slopes
With their surface fragrance of thyme and beneath
A secret system of caves and conduits; hear these springs
That spurt out everywhere with a chuckle.

W.H. Auden, *In Praise of Limestone*

LIMESTONE AND CHALK

The limestone and chalk landscapes are some of the most loved in Britain, yet gardening on them has often been thought disadvantaged. Their soil is alkaline and often poor, limiting the variety of plants that can be grown. Yet they support a wealth of gardens unsurpassed in delicacy and beauty that must be an inspiration to anyone.

The undulating chalk downlands contrast with the older, rockier lands of limestone, but geologically and chemically they are similar. Both bear the same type of flora, and the term limestone technically embraces chalk. Laid down in tropical seas and lakes 100 million to over 200 million years ago, the limestones are the residue of countless billions of blue-green algae – 'nano-planktons' – which sank to the seabed with other creatures. An electron micrograph of chalk shows a mass of minuscule sea anemones and snails. The earlier limestones are composed of about 50 per cent calcium carbonate, sometimes much more, while the later chalk is nearly 98 per cent calcium carbonate.

LIME LANDSCAPE

The most ancient limestone is the grey mountain or Carboniferous (the latter name because it is found in association with the coal measures) limestone of Cumbria, Northumberland, parts of Yorkshire, Wales and the Mendips, and so folded and pressured that it makes dramatic landscapes with crags and rocky clefts like the Cheddar Gorge. It is the karst landscape of Auden's poem. The later, honey-coloured dolomitic or magnesian limestone runs south from Durham via Yorkshire to Nottingham. The oolitic limestone laid down in Jurassic times – fossilized dinosaur footprints have been found in quarries near Swanage – runs from the Isle of Purbeck in Dorset through the Cotswolds and in a swath across the country to Yorkshire; this has produced some of the finest buildings in the country, from Wells Cathedral in Somerset to York Minster. Other types of limestone, such as Kentish ragstone, appear to a lesser degree; outcrops occur in Scotland and Ireland, where the pavement of the Burren is famed for its wild flowers, as well as being a major component around the Mediterranean, in Greece, Turkey, the Pyrenees, the mountains of western China, the coast of western Australia and many places elsewhere. It is hardly surprising that so many Mediterranean trees, shrubs and bulbs flourish in limy soils. Marine fossils, the most common being spiralled ammonites integral to the stone and on the Isle of Purbeck chipped out to adorn the walls, are found in all limestones.

OPPOSITE PAGE:
The chalk and lime regions of England and Wales.

Fossil ammonites found in limestone.

Limestone is porous, and rain runs to the weakest places and sinks, in mountain limestone creating underground caves such as Wookey Hole and Ingleborough Cave, leaving on the surface crags, rocks and fissured pavements in which little soil remains. At Parcevall Hall in Yorkshire plants are grown in pockets of soil left in the rough limestone slope. In the softer, oolitic limestone, more akin to chalk, water sinks through the stone and works its way sideways and down through the weaker points until it finds an impermeable clay layer and subsequently reaches the surface in springs.

CHALK

Softest and youngest of the limestones, the chalk stretches broad fingers from a hub in the Salisbury Plain, south-west to Dorset, north-east across the country to Norfolk, Lincolnshire and Yorkshire, and eastwards to the North and the South Downs. From Kent the chalk stretches into northern France, Germany and beyond.

All limestone is porous, but chalk being the softest is the most porous of all. On chalk the water is absorbed, so a hill becomes a sponge where the water level rises or sinks according to the rainfall. Many valley streams start to flow weeks after rainwater has percolated down to springs. The chalk's porosity, whereby water is sucked up by capillary action, allows trees and shrubs to survive in times of apparent drought, for, unlike sand, it never entirely dries out.

In the chalk the commonest fossils are flint sea urchins, locally called 'shepherds crowns' or 'fairy loaves' and formerly kept in dairies to prevent milk magically from turning sour. As the Cretaceous seas settled, the silica in them fused to form flint fossils and stones, and today they lie in layers along their chalk matrix. They can be seen along the cliffs of Beer in Devon or down the flint mines of Grime's Graves in Norfolk.

Chalk downland in spring, with introduced birch and cherry.

Chalk downland seen from the gardens of Hinton Ampner, Hampshire, in July.

BUILDING

The lands of limestone and chalk were some of the earliest inhabited in Britain, and the area of Salisbury Plain with its ancient trackways, hilltop camps, tumuli and stone monuments shows more signs of continuous early occupation than almost any other. The lighter vegetation of these uplands was easier to clear than that of the marshy lowlands, and their dryness in all weathers made them natural causeways, from Kent to Wiltshire, and from Wiltshire across to East Anglia on the ancient Ridgeway. Evidence of the earliest farming lies in ridge and furrow lines on limestone and chalk lands, across the Dorset hills and elsewhere. Flints were used, chipped to form axes, knives and arrowheads in the days before iron. At Grime's Graves over 366 shafts worked by antler picks and ox shoulder-blade shovels were dug to bring up and export the flints embedded in the chalk. The Roman villas of ancient Britain, built long before the Anglo-Saxons came to drain the clay lowlands, are mostly scattered over chalk and limestone country. Their inhabitants appreciated the good drainage and lack of flooding.

Limestone towns and villages stamp the landscape with a unique character. The dour, grey villages of

the West Riding of Yorkshire, their garden walls often adorned with bizarre lumps of twisted mountain limestone like abstract sculpture, the golden villages of mid Yorkshire built from magnesian limestone, the much visited Cotswold cream villages of oolitic limestone, the buff-coloured towns of Oxfordshire, the warm, grey villages of Dorset, the nearly white castles of Portland all bear witness to the underlying structure of the land. Most limestone is tough but soft enough to work, and the stones from different strata are used for carving, splitting into roof slates, rubble filling, walls or the drystone walls of fields and gardens. The architecture of successive centuries is linked by the same stone, its colour and texture varying from quarry to quarry, used for church, house, barn and cottage, and, despite modern needs and traffic, it still reflects a culture at one with its environment.

The towns and villages on chalk are more varied and their underlying base is less obvious. Brick, baked from the nearest clay, has been the predominant building material for the last three centuries. Nevertheless, chalk and flint have been and still are used. Chalk, like limestone, is not uniform in consistency; in some places it is sufficiently hard to be quarried as 'clunch' and used as building stone. The Elizabethan Loseley House in Surrey has stone rubble

Limestone house in Oxfordshire, with climbing roses 'Mme Alfred Carrière' and 'Cécile Brunner'.

walls with whitewashed clunch dressings, and at Old Ditcham Farm in Hampshire a beautiful eighteenth-century barn, as uplifting as any church, survives with enormous pointed arches of malm, a form of chalk; Ashdown Park in Berkshire is built of chalk with brown stone dressings. Most chalk is too soft to be cut as building blocks, although it is often used in church interiors where its softness makes for ease of carving, as witnessed by the elaborate foliage of the chalk interior at the Lady Chapel of Ely Cathedral.

The true stone of chalk is the embedded flint, hard and unforgiving. The Romans used it to build castle walls. Later churches were built of it. Smaller churches are built of undressed flints, giving walls a soft appearance like grey cardboard, and sometimes plastered over. In Norfolk the tower is often round, saving the necessity of importing more easily worked stone for the corners. Grander churches are built of dark flints, with their outer faces knapped and squared, giving them an austerity as they glassily throw back the light. In Norfolk and Suffolk elaborate flint flushwork, patterned combinations of knapped flint and stone forming chequers, lozenges, blank arcading and monograms, decorates walls and towers like large-scale jewellery. The quoins, cornerstones, jambs and mullions, like the entire body of any cathedral worth its salt, are always imported stone.

The earliest cottages in chalk villages are usually timber framed, or cob, where packed chalk, straw and small flints have been pugged between boards, left to dry and later plastered. Later, brick was introduced, and more flint cottages and houses were built. Here, play with the two materials makes for fascinating variation. Because flint is so hard to work, as with the churches the dressings are constructed of brick or stone. Cley-next-the-Sea in Norfolk has a mass of flint houses with rosy brick dressings. In Wiltshire brick and flint bands, chequer patterns of stone and flint, and courses of rounded flint pebbles are just some of the forms around. Occasionally a cottage is built, cornerstones and all, of unknapped flint, giving it the look of a grotto. Plenty of great houses are built of limestone, but few from flint, although Goodwood House makes a noble try. Roofs are tiled, thatched or slate. Despite their often considerable charm, the towns and villages of the chalklands lack the cohesion and unity with the landscape of those on limestone.

Garden walls in chalk country are often flint topped by coping bricks. Another familiar type is

TOP LEFT: *Chalk ashlar and flints used for the walls of Marsh Court, Hampshire, designed in 1901 by Edwin Lutyens.*

TOP RIGHT: *Flint and brick terrace house in Hampshire, with roses 'New Dawn' and 'American Pillar'.*

ABOVE LEFT: *Cathedral gateway, Norwich, with flushwork of knapped flints and stone.*

ABOVE MIDDLE: *St George Tombland, Norwich, with flushwork of knapped flints on porch, and flint chequerwork on tower.*

ABOVE RIGHT: *House with brick, limestone and flintwork in Wilton, Wiltshire.*

RIGHT: *House in Wilton, with a medley of old materials including flint and limestone.*

cob, which can survive a considerable time provided that the walls are topped with thatch or tiled coping to prevent erosion by rain. Flint and cob provide an excellent backdrop for roses and climbing plants; brick, particularly bright orange brick, can overwhelm certain colours although it shows up creams and yellows very well.

NATIVE FLORA

The vegetation of limestone and chalk country is light and delicate, with roots that can work their way through rubble and sideways and down through the layers below. The alkaline soil, packed with calcium, supports specific plants. Patchworks of beech, ash, maples and yew grow on the South Downs, and on the downland north of Chichester grows the remnant of a yew forest, and to walk on the fall of needles, unbroken by other plants, is like being under the sea. The ferns of alkaline country are hart's tongue and the rustyback found on the north walls of churches, while the hedges are hawthorns, dog roses, dogwoods, privet, spindleberry and little maples, woven through with old man's beard or traveller's joy, our native clematis. These, like the

Plastered cob wall, on brick base, composed of pugged chalk, stones and straw topped by tile coping, in Hampshire.

Downland with beech trees and cowslips in spring.

Spindleberries in autumn, Euonymus europaeus.

Blue gromwell, Lithospermum purpurocaerulum, *a rare, shade-loving chalk native.*

wayfaring tree – the shrub *Viburnum lantana* – stood on ancient trackways. John Gerard in his *Herball* of 1597 wrote, 'This tree groweth in most hedges in rough and stonie places, upon hils and lower woods, especially in the chalkie grounds about Cobham, Southfleet and Gravesend, and all the tract to Canterburie.' We can imagine pilgrims on their way to Canterbury, enjoying the viburnum and traveller's joy, of which Gerard says, 'These plants have no use in Phisicke as yet found out but are esteemed onely for pleasure by reason of the goodly shadow they make with their thicke bushing and clyming, as also of the beautie of the flowers.'

Anyone who has walked in August the limestone pavements and scarps of Yorkshire, the Peak District and the Burren in Ireland or the undulating downland of Sussex, sees a mass of wild flowers at a time when many gardens on richer soils appear distinctly tired. Harebell, marjoram, bloody cranesbill, rock roses, scabious, centaury and wild carrot are in bloom. Earlier there are bird's-foot-trefoil, pinks and many more. Not only that, but the limestone landscape is rich in wildlife, playing host to butterflies such as the Adonis blue.

Sweet-briar, sainfoin, the autumn gentian, calamint, knapweed, teasel, the clustered bellflower, chalk milkwort and viper's bugloss are just some natives found on lime and chalk and, while their more glamorous cultivars take centre stage in the garden, are worth their place in the wings. Growing some rarities, like the attractive, shade-loving, blue gromwell, will help to save them from extinction.

GARDENS

The walled area of the Oxford Botanic Garden, founded in 1621 so that medical students could learn the taxonomy of physic plants, is the oldest garden in the British Isles, with its basic design virtually unchanged. This alkaline garden contains over 8,000 species and varieties of plants, and holds a National Collection of *Euphorbia*. Ninety per cent of the plant families are found, from the lowest moss and liverworts to the highest orchid and composites – the daisy family. Only in the twentieth century did the University acquire the arboretum of

Nuneham Courtenay to grow lime-hating plants such as rhododendrons, Japanese maples, heathers, camellias and certain rare Chilean shrubs.

Traditionally, a limy or chalk soil was not considered a disadvantage. In *The English Gardener*, William Cobbett wrote,

> chalky soil may make a very good garden; for chalk never burns in summer, and is never wet in winter; that is to say, it never causes stagnant water. It absorbs it, and retains it, until drawn upwards by the summer sun. And hence it is that the chalky downs are fresh and green, while even the meadows in the valleys are burned up so as to be perfectly brown. No tree rejects chalk; chalk is not apt to produce canker in trees; and, upon the whole, it is not a bad soil even for a garden, while, if it have a tolerable depth of earth on the top of it, it is, taking all things together, the pasturage, the sound roads, the easy cultivation in all weathers, the healthiness which it invariably gives …, the very best land in the world.

Cobbett was writing in 1838, years before gardens such as Exbury, Nymans, Leonardslee, Bodnant and Inverewe opened their arms to the ericaceous riches of the east, when plant hunters sent back the seed of not only rhododendrons and azaleas, but camellias, pieris, Japanese maples and much more. In Edwardian times a gardener like Gertrude Jekyll felt that a garden without rhododendrons was hardly worth its name, and her remedy for alkaline soils was to order yet more cartloads of peat. When Sir Frederick Sterne started his famous garden in a chalk pit at Highdown in 1909 a leading nurseryman (he does not say who) told him that nothing would grow there.

Times have changed. The great rhododendron gardens still have their place, but these days the show gardens of Chelsea focus on other plants, and a first-time gardener such as Prince Charles, reared on the acid grounds of Sandringham and Balmoral, chose the alkaline soil of Highgrove in Gloucestershire. Limestone gardening is not about importing alien soil and laying down layers of impermeable membrane. It is about understanding and feeding the soil. It is about growing plants that enjoy the soil, and about appreciating the particular delicacy and lightness that the calcicoles – alkaline lovers – bring.

CHAPTER 1

Soil

The amount of nutrient in the soil is not necessarily a good guide to what is available to the plant growing in it. This is determined by the soil's acidity or alkalinity. All limestone contains varying levels of calcium, causing alkalinity. On the domestic front, water from calcium-containing areas is hard, furring up taps and kettles. In the garden, calcium is toxic to several plants including nearly all the ericaceous family – rhododendrons, andromedas, *Pieris* and most heathers.

The alkalinity or acidity of the soil is measured by its pH, a logarithmic measure of the hydrogen ion concentration,[1] with values from 1 (most acidic) to 14 (most alkaline), thus a soil of 8.1 is ten times as alkaline as 7.1. The greatest alkalinity of chalk and lime soils is about 8.5. A glass of pure water is neutral, with a pH of 7; anything lower is acid, and anything higher is alkaline. Rainwater is slightly acid – or soft. Soils vary from pH 5.5 in acid soils to 8.5 in alkaline soils. The optimum pH for growing the widest variety of plants is 6.5, slightly below neutral.

5.5	strongly acid
5.5–5.9	medium acid
6.0–6.4	slightly acid
6.5–6.9	very slightly acid
7.0	neutral
7.1–7.5	very slightly alkaline
7.6–8.0	slightly alkaline

OPPOSITE PAGE: *Marsh orchids in grass beside pond. Eight years previously the pond was excavated; no top soil was added to the chalk detritus, but a small amount of grass seed was scattered and within seven years marsh orchids arrived among the fine grass; the pH of this soil is well over 8.5.*

RIGHT: *The pond in the preceding illustration shortly after excavation, showing the bare chalk; the pond is fed by natural springs.*

[1] For the technically minded: the formula is given by $pH = \log_{10}(1/[H^+])$, where $[H^+]$ is the hydrogen ion concentration. The fact that this appears as a reciprocal in the formula is the explanation for high acidity being linked to a low pH and high alkalinity to a high pH. The scale was devised by the Danish chemist Søren Sørensen in 1909; the p in pH is from the Danish *potenz*, strength.

| 8.1–8.5 | medium alkaline |
| 8.5 | strongly alkaline |

The alkalinity of the soil may vary in any garden, and the underlying stone does not necessarily indicate the pH of the soil above. Large areas of Norfolk and Suffolk are composed of chalk that was strewn with acid sand of varying depths during the Ice Ages. The chalk comes to the surface in some places naturally and in others where pits have been dug for liming or flints quarried for building, as at the Plantation Garden in Norwich. In southern England the chalk downlands with alkaline soil often bear clay caps with acid deposits which can support colonies of plants such as camellias and azaleas reluctant to grow on adjacent ground. Rivers through alkaline country often leave deposits of an acid or neutral nature – the water garden of Longstock with adjacent azaleas on the chalk River Test is one. In Yorkshire areas of limestone and chalk are strewn with debris of varying pH left from the Ice Ages.

ALKALINE SOILS

Typical alkaline soils in chalk and limestone country are like porridge in colour and drain rapidly after rain. They are usually full of stones, but light and comparatively easy to fork.

Alkaline clay, where the soil is baked hard and almost impossible to dig in dry summers and a sticky mess in winter, is a different matter. Nori and Sandra Pope faced alkaline clay with a high pH when they took over Hadspen Gardens in Somerset. For ten years they brought in an annual 150 tons of farmyard manure and spread it over nearly half a mile of flower and shrub borders. Some clay gardeners recommend adding gravel, but Nori Pope says that this is a recipe for concrete and that coarse, strawy farmyard manure is vastly better for achieving a workable soil. The results at Hadspen speak for themselves, where some of the most beautiful borders in the country, unwatered, stand unwilting after weeks without rain.

NUTRIENTS

The main nutrients a plant needs are nitrogen (N) for leaf growth, phosphorus (P) for root growth, and potassium (K) for fruiting. In a general fertilizer such as Growmore the composition is shown as NPK 7-7-7, indicating that the proportion of each element is

Flints with natural holes, dug from the garden and strung on a pole as sculpture; other flints can be used to edge paths, as foundations for paths or with lime mortar for building flint walls.

7 per cent by weight. In a tomato or other fruiting booster the potassium content is greater than that of the others. All these nutrients are widely spread in both acid and alkaline soils, but in alkaline ones the phosphorus becomes unavailable to the calcifuges – the lime haters. Other minor but essential nutrients, particularly iron (Fe) and manganese (Mn), involved in the manufacture of chlorophyll, but also boron (B), zinc (Zn) and copper (Cu) become increasingly unavailable to many plants as the soil's pH rises. Leaf yellowing, veining and scorching, small new foliage, the death of leaves and small branches result. Such a plant has chlorosis.

Only recently has the question been solved of how the calcicoles – lime lovers – obtain iron and manganese from soils where these elements appear inaccessible. The answer is that they create their own acidity by secreting citric and oxalic acid in roots through an intimate relationship with mycorrhizal fungi in the soil. Citric acid dissolves iron and manganese, and oxalic acid dissolves phosphorus, allowing the plants to imbibe them.

SOIL TESTING

It is important to know the exact degree of alkalinity of the soil and to test different parts of the garden to ascertain any variation in pH. An alkaline garden may well have a lower pH or a neutral patch where some calcifuges can be risked.

Several kits are available for the measurement of the pH. The easiest to use is a soil pH meter, a probe pushed into moist soil which, after a minute, indicates the pH on a dial. Readings tend to fluctuate, and the meter is not quite as accurate as a pH testing kit. This involves a bit of chemistry, mixing the reagent, which may be a powder or a liquid, with a sample of soil. Once mixed and allowed to settle, the solution develops a colour that can be compared with a colour chart supplied with the kit to indicate the pH of the soil. A red solution indicates an acid soil, orange is slightly acid, green is neutral while shades of blue indicate alkaline soil. This is an excellent indicator, and good for making comparisons of several soils, but not for the colour blind who can resort to a friend or spouse, or use a pH service provided by the RHS and *Gardening Which*.

IMPROVING THE SOIL

Can the basic pH of the soil be altered? A little. Adding lime is the traditional method of raising the pH of acid soils. In the 3 acres of the new Winter Garden at the Sir Harold Hillier Arboretum 1,000 tons of alkaline soil improver were added to the acid soil; the alkalinity of the soil was raised by about 2 per cent, although with time that lessened. Likewise, adding neutral compost to alkaline soil slightly lower the pH over the years. Flowers of sulphur or ammonium sulphate fertilizer added to soil lowers the pH and can be useful in kitchen gardens if added a month before sowing; these are less effective in soils containing particles of free chalk or limestone. Gardens on hard limestone, particularly those worked for decades or even longer tend to be less alkaline and able to grow a wider range than gardens on chalk where the soft calcium from the soil's bedrock is continually dissolving and thwarting efforts to ameliorate its alkalinity. Most chalk gardens maintain a consistently high pH.

The yellowing leaves of plants deprived of iron and other nutrients owing to the soil's alkalinity can to some extent be remedied by a twice yearly dose of Sequestrene, Miracid or some similar agent, although in chalky soil the extra iron soon gets locked away. Such agents may be usefully applied when a young plant, say wisteria or *Photinia* 'Red Robin', is looking pallid while getting established, but once it is mature it should be unnecessary. Applying sequestered iron to keep acid lovers alive in alkaline soils is an expensive and pointless exercise.

Amateur kits for measuring soil nutrients are not as yet that reliable, and, rather than randomly dosing the soil for possible deficiencies, it is better to increase its health and moisture retention though the addition of compost. It may seem, looking at pasty soil, that added compost has disappeared, but over the years the soil's fertility will be greatly increased. Compost promotes earthworm activity and boosts the essential partnership between soil, mycorrhizal fungi and plants, and increases moisture retention. Even if the pH of the soil is not significantly lowered, it will be able to support a wider range of plants; well worked gardens achieve a most desirable soil, well drained yet moist and supporting all but the most chauvinistic calcifuges.

COLOUR

Flowers have evolved as modified leaves, so it is hardly surprising that the chemistry of the soil affects their colour. On alkaline soils some roses are less saturated in tone. The blue Himalayan poppy *Meconopsis betonicifolia* instead of flowering a clear, light blue becomes pale mauve on alkaline soils, and hydrangeas bloom pink rather than blue. However, blue flowers such as *Anchusa* are as rich in tone as ever. It is a question of trial and observation. Acid lovers such as Japanese maples grow into pleasing shrubs on alkaline soils with a depth of humus, but their autumn colour is usually less intense.

Pasty-coloured, alkaline soils do not show up small, pale flowers – in this case a pink squill – to advantage; here bright blue or pink would show up better.

COMPOST

Many plants do not object to alkalinity so much as the dry conditions which usually come with it. To some extent this can be remedied by the application of compost to the soil. Well-rotted farmyard manure is the classic one, and, if it is available, well and good. If there is a mushroom farm nearby cheap supplies of spent mushroom compost may be obtainable. This is often chalk based, and although compounding the problems of alkalinity, it contains the essential humus and is better than nothing. Bagged farmyard manure, concentrated chicken manure and a wide range of commercial composts all help the soil.

The cheapest soil improver is home compost. Digging spadefuls of compost from former detritus is as satisfying as gathering vegetables from what was a packet of seeds. Composting lets us into the cycle of decay and regeneration as thousands of flies, slugs, worms, microbes and fungi weave into kitchen and garden waste, transforming it to dark loam. It is not high in nutrients, but that does not matter. The soil has the nutrients. The compost can be laid on or dug into the soil, put into containers for bulbs and other plants, applied to lilies or used with a handful of fish, blood and bone, or bonemeal, when planting trees and shrubs.

For the compost heap in a large or medium-sized garden, the traditional method is to build three bays from wire netting or pallets; these can be bought as modular wooden bins with sliding panels for easy access. The first bay has fresh material, the second has material decomposing and the third supplies the compost to be dug into the garden. A sunny spot is ideal, but a shady corner is adequate. From the house, all vegetable and fruit peelings, the contents of the vacuum cleaner, eggshells, egg boxes and the cores of toilet rolls can go in. From the garden, virtually all vegetable material is acceptable, excepting woody prunings. It is like making a cake with layers of different ingredients, balanced with moist and dry; compost with nothing but dry material cannot decompose, and with nothing but orange peel becomes sodden and spongy. If a heap gets too wet, oxygen levels become depleted and anaerobic decomposition occurs. This is not as good as the usual aerobic decomposition because it is a slower process and the material is not subjected to the higher temperatures required to kill off seeds and diseases.

Pile the heap high because it compacts over the months. When completed, the heap can be covered with plastic sheeting or an old carpet to retain its moisture. Turning the compost speeds the process, but is unnecessary. In ten months or sooner everything will have rotted to a dark mass smelling of damp woodland. Often the top of the heap is dry and unrotted while the base is ready for collection. Place the top in the current collecting bay and fork out the rest.

A word of warming: avoid adding leftover pieces of meat, cheese and bread, which attract rats and other vermin. Go slow on evergreen clippings since they take a long time to decompose. Avoid dog or cat litter. However, the manure of vegetarian pets, such as guinea pigs or rabbits, is fine mixed with straw. Newspapers are best recycled in council skips or collected by recycling lorries. Most weeds are excellent in the compost bin since the temperature usually rises to about 65°C (149°F), hot enough to kill most seeds and diseases. However, the roots of bindweed, creeping buttercup and couch grass should be put in the dustbin or burnt. It is too annoying if they survive to infect other parts of the garden.

For small gardens there are several options. The simplest composter is like a dustbin without a base. Many local councils, in order to reduce the infill burden on their tips, provide these free or at a subsidized rate and it is worth enquiring whether this applies in your area. This composter should be sited in a sunny corner on bare earth so that earthworms can enter and help the process. The lid is lifted and inside goes all organic kitchen waste and garden debris. Occasionally the top layer may be mixed into the lower. In warm weather there is a slight rotting smell when the lid is lifted, but nothing virulent. Within a year the bottom layer is rotted, dark, crumbly, wet smelling, riddled with pink earthworms and perfect for use in the garden. The only awkwardness arises in tipping up the bin, taking compost from the base and getting the bin straight again.

The most convenient small composter is one which works on the same principle as the bottomless dustbin but has hatch doors at the base for shovelling out ripe material. It is an on-going process, fresh

Russian comfrey, Symphytum caucasicum, *beside gold marjoram; comfrey can spread, but is excellent as an accelerator on compost heaps. Picked and placed in a bucket with a lid, it rots down and the resulting liquid, although unpleasant to smell, is a good liquid feed which can be applied diluted to house plants, container plants and crops generally.*

waste going on top and compost pulled out from below. Composters of this type, made from plastic or wood, are available from catalogues and garden centres. The best plastic ones have air vents which allow a degree of aeration – essential for successful composing. Some of the wooden composters come in the form of beehives and can create a focal point at the end of the garden.

Wormeries produce the caviare of composts, the finest and blackest of all. The wormery is a large,

The Herb Society's show garden at Chelsea 2003 included a decorative beehive; composters in the form of beehives are widely available and can be used in small gardens.

plastic bin with a hinged lid, a drainage platform inside near the base and beneath this a tap. Compost and worms are placed on the platform, and then household and garden wastes are added gradually. The worms slowly munch through the debris, turning it into black loam. Liquid is collected at the base and poured from the tap, where it is used as an additional fertilizer. However, managing a wormery successfully is an art that requires practice, care and attention, and the worms tend to have an unacceptably high death rate.

Also available is the tumble composter, a rotating barrel on a frame. This is for those wanting compost in a hurry, and the secret lies in rotating it daily, which distributes moisture and builds up a central heat core. In goes the rubbish, a mix of household and garden wastes, the lid is screw on and each day the capstan handle is turned. After twenty-one days

it produces a decent, rough compost suitable for digging into the soil. The plus is, it works, and it works quickly. Among the minus points is the fact that, since waste is continually accumulating, you need a large collection bin while the tumbler is turning. If you choose this method, Blackwalls's Compost Tumbler swings on a frame, making it easier to fill and empty, and the new Envirocycle is a neat, plastic drum small enough to fit on a balcony.

Leaves take longer to break down than other garden detritus. The traditional method of disposal was the bonfire, hardly an option today. If you have a massive supply of autumn leaves, place them in a separate bay or plastic bin liners. Left undisturbed over two years the leaves from prunus, beech, catalpa, horse chestnut and the like rot into a fruitcake consistency. If you have only a few leaves, they may be added to a general compost heap of trimmings

A wooden butt from a wine barrel in the corner of a garden, with the male fern, Dryopteris felix-mas.

and cuttings, with layers of grass mowings. Alternatively, leaves may be left where they lie on flower beds, to be pulled below by worms. Leaf mould, with its low nutrient level, is invaluable for potting up lilies and plants which dislike too rich a medium.

General compost accelerators, as well as specialist accelerators for grass and leaves, are available in liquid or granular form; these harness microbes and enzymes to speed the breakdown process. However, since decomposition is inevitable they are hardly essential.

Grass clippings produce a slimy mess on their own, and are best layered with household and other garden wastes.

When the compost is added to the garden, some weed seeds may have survived. If home compost is used in containers, most weed seeds are suppressed if the top 4cm is covered with sterilized, commercial compost. In the greenhouse, commercial seed compost is the most convenient one to use. The only way to ensure that home compost is seed-free is to bake it in the oven or use a soil sterilizer; the latter with a capacity of 34ltr costs about £300.

WATERING

Watering in dry summers while establishing trees and shrubs is essential in limy and chalky soils. A tap connected to a leaky hose and delivering a steady trickle works wonders. However, these buried hoses are useless in the vegetable or flower border where they become, inevitably, forked and punctured. Taps attached to the mains are useful for sprinklers, but in these days of hot summers and water shortages the aim must be to keep regular watering at a minimum by planting material that when mature is not going to droop and die in times of drought.

Water butts are invaluable when placed at strategic places round the house. Plastic ones are serviceable, but come in ugly greens. Lead tanks are smart but expensive, while costing less are plastic tanks in imitation lead. Wooden butts look pleasing in any garden.

The best time to plant anything is when the soil is damp. Good times are autumn and spring, and in summer after or during a rainy period.

CHOOSING PLANTS FOR ALKALINE SOIL

Gardeners on lime or chalk must bear in mind two considerations when choosing plants. The first is whether the plants can tolerate or enjoy an alkaline soil. The second, for those with a typical soil which seems perpetually parched, is whether they can tolerate dry conditions.

CHAPTER 2

Trees

Trees are the bones of the garden, the long-term investment. On either side of a view they enhance and can even create it, in front of a pylon they hide it; carefully placed a tree becomes a focal point. Trees are for shade, colour, flower and winter outline, they are for birds to roost and nest in, and larders for insects. The mature trees of today were planted by generations who can only have imagined their present impact. The fact that some trees may reach their full height and splendour only when we are gone should never deter us at any age from planting.

LARGE TREES

When choosing a tree, bear in mind its eventual height. Although trees can be kept in bounds by pollarding and pruning, they should be allowed to reach for the skies.

Most trees, even if content on a thin, alkaline topsoil, do not reach the height as they would in richer conditions. But there are exceptions which come close to their counterparts on benign neutral soil. One of the finest is the common beech, *Fagus sylvatica*, our downland native. John Evelyn (1662) wrote in *Sylva* how the beech makes 'noble shades with their well furnished and glistening leaves.' In the valleys they grow to a 'stupendious procerity, though the soyl be stony and very barren. Also upon the declivities, sides and tops of high Hills and Chalkie Mountains especially; for they will strangely insinuate their roots into the bowels of those seemingly impenetrable places.' Nothing is lovelier than the light green, pleated leaves emerging in spring and creating an aquarium setting below, their dark green in summer, the ripeness of their autumn colour and the elephant smoothness of the bark in winter. The fern or cut-leaved beech, *F. s.* var. *heterophylla* 'Asplenifolia', with serrated, lobed leaves, gives an effect like those feathery trees framing distant views in paintings by Claude. It comes in several forms, displaying leaves variously cut and

OPPOSITE PAGE:
Tibetan cherry, Prunus serrula, *in winter with deer protection.*

RIGHT: *Copper beech and* Catalpa bignonioides *(right).*

Cut-leaved walnut, Juglans nigra *'Laciniata', in Cambridgeshire.*

tinged deep red. Later in the dark green of summer, they have an aromatic scent which becomes pungent when the leaves are crushed. This aroma repels insects and is one reason why in fields cattle love to sit or stand under walnut trees where they are less bothered by flies. The black walnut, *Juglans nigra*, is a noble tree with large leaves producing plenty of nuts; *J. n.* 'Laciniata' is a lovely, airy, cut-leaved form with long, scalloped leaflets, barely recognizable as a walnut yet still producing nuts. A good, all-purpose walnut is the compact *J. regia* 'Broadview', extremely precocious and bearing nuts three years after planting. The time to pickle green walnuts is in late June or when the entire fruit can be pierced by a pin. Walnut juice blackens fingers and has been used as ink and a soft grey dye for carpets in Turkey. Squirrels are excessively fond of ripe walnuts, which is why a harvest may vanish overnight, and later seedlings will appear in parts of the garden where a walnut could never have fallen.

The common ash, *Fraxinus excelsior*, is one of our natives and can self-seed to a weed-like extent but it is a magnificent tree in its own right with airy, pinnate leaves, and one of the most valuable for timber. In winter it is easily recognized by its black buds and in spring holds bunches of winged keys. The weeping ash, *F. e.* 'Pendula', grows in a balanced but asymmetrical fashion, and during a winter storm its bare outline sways like a whirling oriental dancer. Its seedlings are that of the common ash. Another good ash is the manna ash, *F. ornus*, medium-sized and flowering in May with a mass of creamy panicles.

The sycamore, *Acer pseudoplatanus*, although a picturesque, large tree which will grow anywhere and survive blasting winds, has received a mixed press as a garden tree. Its leaves are usually spotted with black fungus by midsummer, but this affects only their appearance. They fall early and Evelyn in the seventeenth century complained that they quickly putrefied and marred his walks. It needs a large garden, and, like the ash, its seedlings can become invasive. *A. p.* 'Leopoldii', speckled and splashed yellow and pink before turning green, grows to only three-quarters of the height of *A. pseudoplatanus*. *A. platanoides* 'Drummondii' has pale green leaves with yellow margins, making a pale gold effect, and can be surprisingly vigorous, growing to about 17m.

lobed, and is not widely grown, although it is as easy to establish as the common beech and as beautiful. The copper beech, *F. s. purpurea*, of which one of the best varieties is 'Riversii', grows as high as its green counterpart and is as handsome, the leaves opening a pale khaki and darkening to deepest maroon. The cut-leaved variety, *F. s.* 'Rohanii' is slow growing but a remarkable ornamental. Weeping beeches, and columnar, fastigiate beeches are other beech forms not widely seen.

Walnuts can take a dry, thin soil, and may do better there than in a rich one, because in the latter they can grow too quickly and lushly, bearing young branches later snapped by winter storms. Grown in meaner conditions, they develop slower and become tough. One of their charms is when they come into leaf, the shoots and unfurling leaves

Weeping ash, Fraxinus excelsior *'Pendula', in winter.*

Acer platanoides *'Drummondii'*.

With this, as with all variegated plants, it is necessary to look out for reversion, with shoots growing plain green leaves. They must be cut out otherwise they will grow stronger and become out of balance with the rest of the tree.

A good companion beside a copper beech, and rather lower in height, is the Indian bean tree, *Catalpa bignonioides*, its green leaves looking golden in contrast. It is vigorous and rounded in outline. Its large spade leaves appear so late that they are never affected by late frosts, and in summer give dappled shade. In August, when other trees can be dull, it bears white flowers with dotted lines luring insects inside, and later a mass of pods like frozen rain. It has no autumn colour, its large leaves being blasted by the first frosts, falling and scurrying like black rats on the ground. It is easily raised from seed.

Flower of Catalpa bignonioides, *the Indian bean tree.*

The horse chestnuts, *Aesculus hippocastrum*, from Turkey and Iran are happy on dry, alkaline soils, and are often self-seeding. There is nothing quite like their candelabras in early summer and, although pink- and red-flowered varieties exist, nothing compares with the common white. However, although handsome, horse chestnuts have a certain coarseness and lack of grace, and their total shade makes them unsuitable for any but parks or large gardens. They flower profusely within a year or two of planting, but it is a shame to establish a tree which may become a monster in maturity. In autumn come the conkers like balls of polished mahogany and Richard Mabey suggests that, since their origin is in Turkey, where they are used as medicine for horses, this may be the reason for the horse chestnut name. The Indian chestnut, *A. indica*, is a stunning aristocrat with flowers marked red and yellow which also needs space, but it is less hardy than the common chestnut. For those wanting a chestnut but without the room to grow the common type, *A. pavia* is available, with interesting, coral red flowers opening slightly.

The leaves of false acacia, *Robinia pseudoacacia*, are delicate, pinnate fronds of light green, and after fifty years this tree can make about 17m. In June it attracts bees and drops a mass of white pea flowers like confetti on the lawn. Once established, it can be a nuisance sending up spiny suckers on the lawn. It is gawky in outline, and three in a group look better than a single specimen. *R. p.* 'Umbraculifera' is a small tree with lollipop heads, attractive and unusual when planted as a short avenue leading from one part of the garden to another. It rarely flowers. Limes are splendid in avenues or a group, but, again, in outline not really of great individual beauty. Many, like *Tilia* 'Petiolaris' whose wonderfully scented flowers are poisonous to bees, are disfigured in summer by sooty mould, a sticky black fungus which drops like glue on cars parked beneath. The best choice is the Crimean lime, *T. euchlora*, bearing similar flowers but a fairly clean species without sooty mould.

The best of the birches, and taking fairly dry conditions, is the silver birch, 'the Lady of the Woods', *Betula pendula*. It can be grown as a specimen or in a group of three or five, and looks beautiful in winter with the black and white trunks and the gently weeping, dark red shoots moving in the wind. Bulbs can be grown underneath it.

Then there are those glorious trees which take up to twenty years before producing the effect they were planted for: the tulip tree, *Liriodendron tulipifera*, can sulk for five years before making up its mind to stretch and grow, and a decade before producing its fragrant green and yellow flowers. These, although lovely, are sometimes unnoticed, not being as immediately glamorous as, say, the pocket handkerchief tree. In the meantime, the lobed leaves are attractive in themselves. The pocket handkerchief or dove tree, *Davidia involucrata*, takes years before producing its ghostly white bracts, but is always handsome with its serrated leaves, rather like a hornbeam. In the first year or two it may throw suckers, which must be cut out. Both these trees, when generously planted, flourish on thin alkaline soil.

As well as the doughty warriors which can cope with thin stony soils, a wide variety of larger trees grow well in alkaline conditions as long as they have sufficient moisture and depth of soil, appreciating the good drainage which usually comes with limy conditions. The balsam poplars have foliage smelling of beeswax polish, which is particularly powerful when the young leaves unfurl; a good variety is *Populus × jackii*. It is a medium to tall sized tree. The zelkova elm, *Zelkova carpinifolia*, is a handsome tree, happy in both acid and alkaline soils, slow growing and not widely seen, but with a fine outline and pleated leaves also rather like a hornbeam. It makes a good alternative to the elms, all of which are now prone to the Dutch elm disease beetle. New disease-resistant breeds are being created through breeding and genetic modification and within the decade these should become available.

The hickories from North America, not widely seen, have an upright stance and brilliant yellow autumn colouring. The bitternut hickory, *Carya cordiformis*, grows well on alkaline soil, but in a frost pocket usually comes into leaf too soon and gets blasted; it recovers, sending out a fresh supply of leaves. The tree of heaven, *Ailanthus altissima*, when mature has green-white flowers with a strong, sweet smell not appreciated by everyone, and, like the Indian bean tree, is one of the first trees to drop its leaves in autumn.

MEDIUM AND SMALL TREES

The most widely grown small tree on alkaline soils must be the flowering cherry, but it does have drawbacks. There is a wide variety, but the cherries are not long-lived, rarely lasting longer than twenty years. When mature, they are prone to canker caused by a bacterium producing wilting, dieback, 'shot holing' in leaves and weeping gum on the trunk, which must be pruned and treated with a winter spray of Bordeaux mixture. Almost all the flowering cherries have double blooms and this means, like most double flowers where an excess of petals is achieved at the expense of the flower's fertility, they have no stamens nor style and produce no autumn fruit. They attract no bees or other pollinating insects and there is never that exciting buzz around the blossom that gives another flowering tree that sense of being a sun surrounded by whirling planets. The flowering cherries are in bloom for two weeks or so, but for the rest of the year they are dull, without grace or beauty and usually with a lumpy graft point at the base or the apex of the trunk. However, for sufferers of hay fever, their lack of stamens bearing pollen may be seen as a benefit.

The cherries worth considering are the winter flowering cherry, *Prunus subhirtella autumnalis*, with its dainty blooms of palest pink on a mild winter's day, and the Tibetan cherry, *P. serrula*, with its shining bands of mahogany satin particularly noticeable on a winter's day. *P. padus*, the bird cherry, has long panicles of cream flowers, and *P. sargentii*, with its smooth chestnut bark, single pink flowers and autumn colouring is one of the loveliest of cherries. The purple-leaved cherry, *P. cerasifera pissardii*, lives considerably longer than most of the others and in early March its pale pink blooms contrast with the opening purple leaves. It can throw suckers, which have to be cut back. Portuguese laurel, *Prunus lusitanica*, being evergreen is usually grown as a screening shrub, but it makes a pleasant small tree, with flowers like candles in April and taking a considerable degree of shade. It is hardier and a better choice on dry soils than the common or cherry laurel, *P. laurocerasus*.

Crab apples have two seasons of interest, blossom and later fruit, and are healthier and longer living than most flowering cherries. *Malus* 'John Downie' has a mass of white blossom and later red fruit so bright it looks enamelled, while *M.* × *zumi* 'Golden Hornet' has blossom followed by golden fruit as exotic as Christmas decorations. *M. floribunda* is delicately blossomed white and pink. *M.* × *purpurea* 'Royalty' has wine-red flowers, purple leaves and purple fruit. All the fruit, high in pectin, can be turned into crab apple jelly, or left for the birds. If a tree flowers regularly but produces no fruit, it probably lacks a tree nearby for pollination or is not getting sufficient moisture for the fruit to swell and ripen.

Laburnums are so accommodating that they can be seen, probably self-seeded, on railway embankments in southern England, as well as in gardens everywhere. The long, gold racemes are beautiful in May and the trees can cope with highly alkaline

Malus × purpurea *'Royalty'*.

Flowers of the crab apple tree, Malus × purpurea *'Royalty'*.

Hawthorn, Crataegus laevigata *'Crimson Cloud'*.

soil. Their drawbacks are that, like the cherries, they are not long-living, showing signs of stress after forty years or less, and they are shallow rooting, often needing continual support. The seeds are poisonous, but so are numerous other garden plants – aconites, datura and periwinkle, to name three out of hundreds. *Laburnum* × *watereri* reaches about 4 or 5m after twenty years, and rather smaller with dark leaves is *L. alpinum*.

The hawthorns, natives of lime and chalk country, are some of the oldest cultivated trees. Despite their thorns, they are good garden trees, long-living, compact and healthy. There are sterile double varieties such as *Crataegus laevigata* 'Paul's Scarlet', but better is a fertile, single-flowered variety with five petals, *C. l.* 'Crimson Cloud', with bright red flowers and a white eye. This buzzes with insects when in flower and by autumn bears a mass of red haws. There is

also the cockspur thorn, *C. crus-galli*, with attractive leaves, flowers and fruit, and thorns like needles at a doctor's surgery, and *C. persimilis prunifolia* with the most unhawthornlike leaves which turn a rich autumn colour. The smell of all hawthorn blossom is powerful, in fact, too much for some, and it is perhaps best not grown too near the house. They tolerate clematis twining through the branches, and it is simple to have *M. l.* 'Crimson Cloud' in bloom in May, then covered with the white and purple flowers of *Clematis* 'Venosa Violacea' in July, and finally with the red haws in September. The clematis is cut back and fed each winter.

Another easily grown tree with attractive cream flowers in spring is the snowy mespilus, *Amelanchier lamarckii* from North America. Although often included in lists of lime-haters, it is tolerant of alkaline soils and can fill the gap left by a dead flowering cherry. It is good looking, often but not always bears fruit, and has striking autumn colour.

The Judas tree, *Cercis siliquastrum*, blooms with slate pink pea flowers on pink threads sprouting straight from the branches. Later the kidney-shaped leaves unfurl and a mass of seedpods like rain in still motion develops. It is healthy, long-living and reliable, even if prone to suckering, and as good is the white Judas tree, *C.s.* f. *albida*. When sown its seeds usually germinate, although the offspring of a white Judas tree usually bears pink flowers.

A subtle and rarely grown little tree from North America is the hop tree, *Ptelea trifoliata*, which in June bears small, obscure, yellow-green flowers, nicely scented, and in autumn fruit like gold coins

ABOVE: Crataegus laevigata *'Crimson Cloud', unlike double-flowered varieties, bears hips in autumn.*

ABOVE RIGHT: *Hop tree,* Ptelea trifoliata, *with rock roses below.*

RIGHT: *Flowers of the Judas tree,* Cercis siliquastrum.

or dangling hops. It is one of the hardiest of fragrant trees, accommodating and healthy, and grows to no more than 4m.

Since Vita Sackville-West grew the willow-leaved pear, *Pyrus salicifolia* 'Pendula', for its silver leaves in her White Garden at Sissinghurst, it has been widely planted in white borders and gardens. White blossom in March is followed by the long, grey leaves on weeping branches. Although a small tree, it grows densely and the inner branches can be removed, so that the tree becomes a bower for summer meals. A less widely grown alternative giving the same effect, with small, yellow, scented flowers in June and leaves glistening metallically beneath, is *Eleagnus angustifolia*, although it needs pruning and initial support to become a standard.

LEFT: *Flower and leaf of the white Judas tree,* Cercis siliquastrum *f.* albida.

BELOW LEFT: Pyrus salcifolia *'Pendula'.*

BELOW: Elaeagnus angustifolia *with its small, scented, yellow flowers.*

RIGHT: *The whitebeam,* Sorbus aria, *coming into leaf.*

BELOW RIGHT: *The same whitebeam,* Sorbus aria, *later in flower.*

Trees that have been grown for centuries accrue legends and superstitions which are part of their charm. The May blossom of hawthorn brings disaster to those who carry it indoors; the Judas tree is the tree from which Judas hanged himself; the ash is Yggdrasil, the Norse world tree which props the roof of the sky; to dream of a blasted oak presages death; the rowan, *Sorbus aucuparia,* the fairy tree of Irish myth, in England was planted beside houses as protection against witches. There was a strong taboo against cutting one down, and, when the rowan beside Gavin Maxwell's house near Skye was cursed by the poet Kathleen Raine, he believed it caused the burning of the house and his final illness. Gerard in 1597 called the rowan a wild ash, although it is no relation, and writes of its girth:

> it groweth to the bignesse of a great mans legge: the leaves be great and long ... the flowers be white, and sweete of smell, and grow in tufts, which do turne into round berries, greene at the first, but when they be ripe of a deepe red colour, and of an unpleasante taste: the branches are as full of juice as the Osier, which is the cause that boies do make pipes of the barke thereof as they do of Willows.

Although growing wild in the more acid soils of Wales, it is happy in highly alkaline soils and its neat habit, flowers and scarlet fruit often persisting (perhaps uninviting to birds) until the following summer make it a first-class tree for medium and small gardens. An excellent species from China is *S. hupehensis,* needing a slightly richer soil, with white berries and pinkish stalks.

The beauty of the whitebeam, *Sorbus aria,* a native of chalk downland where it grows with yew, is not only in spring, when its felted leaves open like a mass of chalice flowers, but through the season, with fluffy white flowers and leaves downy white underneath and yellow in autumn. This tree will grow anywhere in well-drained soil.

The mulberry to grow is the black mulberry, *Morus nigra,* promoted and planted by James I at Hampton

Court to further the English silk industry, although, in fact, silkworms prefer the more tender white mulberry. The black mulberry is architectural, gnarled and picturesque with age, and its blackberry-like fruits are very palatable.

Taller, and in the right place reaching to a considerable height, is *Paulonia tomentosa*, the foxglove tree which bears beautiful mauve flowers in early summer before the leaves. It needs a very sheltered site and the buds are easily damaged by late winter frosts and storms. In colder gardens it often survives, coppiced by frosts and producing huge and pleasant summer leaves.

Eucalypts have no objection to poor dry soils, but many dislike high alkalinity. Two of the ones to try on soils with a pH above 7.5 are *Eucalyptus parvifolia*, with young feathery foliage, and *E. dalrympleana*, with orange shoots and bark patchworked cream, brown and grey. It is worth trying

others because reports suggest that, after initial chlorosis, many species make good growth in highly alkaline conditions.

One of the best small trees to plant for foliage is *Acer pseudoplatanus* 'Brilliantissimum' whose leaves open a striking shrimp pink, later changing to pale yellow-green and finally to green. Unlike some maples this one is happy on alkaline soil, as is the box elder, *A. negundo violaceum*, which in spring lets fall pink or violet, iridescent flower strings like frayed silk. The silver maple, *A. saccharinum*, has beautiful, cut leaves, silvery beneath and becomes a most attractive tree, but without a decent depth of soil it can develop fasciation, a sign of stress where the shoots become flat as if pressed through a mangle.

In summer we visit other gardens, but, since we see our own all year round, we must consider a tree's winter dress. The paper bark maple, *Acer griseum*, has curling bark like old paper and like the

Honey locust, Gleditsia triacanthus *'Sunburst', with rose 'Golden Showers'.*

Tibetan cherry, *Prunus serrula*, with its bands of satin bark is particularly noticeable in winter. So is the birch *Betula utilis* var. *jacquemontii*, a medium-sized tree with white bark, best sited where it gleams in the winter sun.

Hornbeams, *Carpinus betulus*, medium- to large-sized trees, can cope with poor soils, waterlogged soils, indeed any soil at all, and are pleasing with their manicured habit and the crowns growing to neat spheres or ovoids.

If a golden-leaved tree is sought, perhaps as a golden wedding present, bear in mind that it will not grow to the same height as its green-leaved counterpart; this may be a useful factor. The golden Indian bean tree, *Catalpa bignonioides* 'Aurea', is stunning from a distance, particularly with the setting sun behind it. Its only disadvantage is that during hot weather the leaves may get scorched. *Robinia pseudoacacia* 'Frisia' is a rich golden-leaved tree, perfect for small gardens, but, being beautiful, easy to grow and well-mannered, it has been widely planted and fallen victim to garden snobbery. Like pampas grass, glorious in its native habitat, it is just too amenable, and gardeners are easily bored. An alternative is the honey locust, *Gleditsia triacanthus* 'Sunburst', which soon becomes a striking, gold tree with small, pinnate leaves.

Oaks are not the trees of alkaline country, particularly on thin soil, because their roots delve deeper than those of the beech or the cherry. Anyone who remembers the devastation of storms in the 1980s can recall beeches overturned entire, their shallow roots spread like pancakes; but the oaks were twisted, wrenched in half by the power of the storms, but rarely uprooted. Nevertheless, with decent planting oaks can reach a satisfying height on alkaline soils, and on thinner soils one of the best to plant is the vigorous Turkey oak, *Quercus cerris*. The evergreen holm oak, *Q. ilex*, takes alkaline soils with aplomb and slowly grows into a sizeable tree. The sweet chestnut, *Castanea sativa*, is not related to the horse chestnut, and, although it will grow satisfactorily in a reasonably deep topsoil, becoming a small- to medium-sized tree, really needs a more neutral soil to flower and fruit well.

If the soil has good depth and is not too highly alkaline, one the more vigorous varieties of the palm-leaved maple, *Acer japonicum*, may be tried, and will

The golden bean tree, Catalpa bignonioides *'Aurea'*.

make a good showing as a shrub, although its autumn colouring is less brilliant than on more acid soils. Norfields, *Acer* specialists of Llangwm Arboretum in Monmouthshire, noticed a dramatic improvement in autumn colour when they moved their nursery from an alkaline soil to one with a lower pH. Although there are exceptions, plants from Japan, New Zealand and Chile, lands of fire and brimstone, tend to be happier in more acid soils.

CONIFERS

After years of being seen as heavy relics from Victorian times, conifers are coming in from the cold. The foliage of many is aromatic, making them a

Picea likiangensis. *In May the new shoots of this spruce are tipped with striking red buds.*

delight to cut when grown as hedging. They are crisp, reliable, usually evergreen, they come in all sizes and there is never the autumn chore of raking, blowing, collecting and carrying leaves. Even the larch, *Larix decidua*, one of the few deciduous conifers, a light haze of green in spring and gold in autumn, sheds such fine needles that they are soon dispersed by winds. It can make a good specimen tree in an alkaline soil of some depth.

Yew, *Taxus baccata*, a native of the chalk downland, can take extremes of alkalinity and acidity, although it is slow to grow as a tree. Among a mass of frothy green growth elsewhere, its dark green leaves strike a contrasting, sober note. Yew is as useful as the columnar Irish yew, *T. b. fastigiata*; its vertical line acting as a punctuation mark in the garden. Two on either side of some steps or a gate, or the entrance to another section of the garden, indicate the approach of new territory. Juniper is another chalk native, and its fastigiate form, *Juniperus scopulorum* 'Skyrocket', with its slim, cypress outline, can perform a similar ushering function in the garden. (So can the box, *Buxus sempervirens* 'Greenpeace' with a pencil-like habit that needs no clipping.) Both yew and juniper once established can take the driest conditions. The cypress, *Cupressus sempervirens*, is the classic, narrow spire familiar in the Mediterranean; tougher than it is usually thought to be, it must be protected from cold winds, particularly in its early years. Good drainage and sun are what it needs.

The dawn redwood, *Metasequoia glyptostroboides*, was known only in fossil form until in the 1940s it was found living in a remote corner of western China and caused a sensation in the botanic world. Conical in shape, turning tawny pink and gold in autumn, it has proved remarkably tolerant of all types of soil. The biggest tree of all, the Wellingtonia, *Sequoiadendron giganteum*, will take an alkaline soil, although another hundred years to pierce the skyline of the surrounding countryside.

Although the spruces, *Picea*, and firs, *Abies*, seem similar, they are unrelated genera, spruces tending to be happier on limy soils than firs. *P. abies*, the Norway spruce, is the standard Christmas tree which, although dreary massed in forests, as a single specimen, providing its base gets sufficient light, makes a good tree with a green crinoline at the base and is highly suitable in season for being spangled with electric lights. *P. likiangensis* looks rather similar, except in May the new shoots are tipped with striking red buds. Later they turn dull, dispensing dusty pollen. *Thuja plicata*, more usually grown as hedging, has a fruity aroma and makes another good-looking conifer.

When it comes to pines, it is best to avoid the five-needled species. Good for chalk and lime soils are our native Scots pine, *Pinus sylvestris*, the Aleppo pine *P. nigra*, which can be useful as a windbreak and does well by the sea, and the lacebark pine, *P. bungea*, a medium-sized pine whose mature bark makes white and black patterns. *P. mugo*, the mountain pine, is a dense, little tree or a small shrub which can take harsh dry conditions.

The maidenhair tree, *Gingko biloba*, is a deciduous conifer which is the sole living survivor of an ancient plant family whose ancestors grew in many areas; it has even been found in fossil form in the London clay. Hardy and happy in all soils, it grows to a medium and eventually to a large tree, and its fan-shaped leaves turn butter-yellow in autumn. Male and female parts occur on separate trees, and it is worth checking that a male rather than a female form is planted because the female fruits when fallen have the foulest smell imaginable, as anyone making an autumn run through New York's Central Park can testify.

The Atlantic Cedar, *Cedrus atlantica* 'Glauca' is easier to establish than the cedar of Lebanon, *C. libani*, and in a larger garden makes a magnificent focal point with its blue-grey foliage. The cedar of Lebanon can also take dry alkaline conditions, as a fine specimen at Hambledon in Hampshire demonstrates, but it does need nursing in its early days. *C. deodara* is a beautiful, slightly weeping cedar and, again, does not object to alkalinity.

The dwarf conifers, with second names such as *nana*, *pumilio*, *pygmaea*, *procumbens* and *compacta* are so called because they grow slowly, but can eventually reach the height of a small tree. One of the best is the bright green *Picea glauca* var. *albertiana* 'Conica', which slowly grows without trimming into a perfect onion dome just over 1m high in fifteen years, perfect at the entrance to a kitchen garden.

DAMP CONDITIONS

Beside water, the willows flourish, including the large weeping willow, *Salix babylonica*, which is eye-catching throughout the year, when about to burst into leaf, during the summer, and the golden falls in autumn. But care needs to be taken with any willow because its roots are invasive, and near the

Picea glauca *var.* albertiana *'Conica', with* Yucca gloriosa *in the background.*

Fairfield House, Hambledon, Hampshire with cedar of Lebanon; the soil here is thin, yet with good planting this tree has flourished.

house they can ensnare and upturn underground pipes. The smaller *S.* 'Chrysocoma' is too often a victim of scab and canker. Best for small gardens and water features is *S. purpurea* 'Pendula', healthier and reaching no more than 3m.

The outline of alder, *Alnus glutinosa*, with old fruit like open cones and little catkins, makes a lacy effect in winter, and a group surrounding a pond is most effective.

Near a pond too, it is worth trying the swamp cypress, *Taxodium distichum*. It likes damp, boggy conditions, and, although frequently labelled as a calcifuge, it is more than tolerant of high alkalinity. This dainty version of the dawn redwood, *Metasequoia glyptostrobes*, to which it is related, when mature is surrounded by woody lumps like gnomes' tables which are pneumatophores, helping the damp roots to breathe.

SITING AND PLANTING

Planting is like sculpture – it has three dimensions. Trees are seen from many angles, and, although their final forms can never be exactly visualized, we can do our best to anticipate a happy juxtaposition. Placing bamboo sticks where trees are going to be planted, walking round and viewing from several angles to see how they interrelate and will be viewed from the house, all help to find the ideal site.

Often, when buying a Judas tree, *Amelanchier* or other tree, a plant with several stems at its base is supplied. If left, it will become a large shrub. To ensure that it grows as a single-trunked standard, on a mild winter's day cut out the lesser of the stems, leaving the strongest to become tree's trunk and leader.

It may seem that one is gaining a march on the years by buying an older tree, but, particularly when trying to establish a plant in dry, stony conditions, the smaller the better. Often when both are planted at the same time the smaller will overtake the larger.

Although trees in containers may be planted at any time of the year, a mild day during the dormant months from October to March is best. The new tree has time to settle before the growing months and roots are rarely in danger of drought. When taking the tree from a container you may find that the roots are pot-bound, spiralling tightly round the base of the pot. At a garden centre you may well want to test and see, gently pulling out a tree to see whether this has happened; if so, avoid the purchase. However, if you are in possession of a pot-bound tree, do not plant it with the roots as they are, because, being habituated to this curling growth, they will continue in the same dwarf-forming manner. Pull the roots out and gently fan them before planting, and with secateurs cut away any that are particularly misshapen.

If a bare-rooted tree arrives during frozen weather or at an unsuitable time, either place it in a pot with damp compost or heel it in somewhere by digging a hole and covering the roots with earth. The essential point is that the roots should never dry out.

Perhaps the most important advice on planting comes from Peter Wake, who gardened on dry downland at Hambledon with a magnificent array of trees, shrubs and roses. He used to say that the ideal size for a hole when planting a tree on solid chalk or lime is a cubic metre, with stony rubble at the base and rough sides for the roots eventually to creep into. This takes some hacking on solid chalk or limestone, and leaves a considerable residue which can be sculptured into a mound or used for constructing a cob or a drystone wall. This hole was then filled with any organic material available, household waste, leaves, grass clippings, none of which was necessarily rotted down. All was shovelled in, and the tree was planted, its roots surrounded by mature compost. He also said that, when the tree's roots reached the fresh organic material, it would have matured to the right consistency, and by the time they reached the chalk or limestone rubble they would be strong enough to penetrate and use the nutrients available. This method may be idealistic, but it makes the point that, particularly in a shallow top soil, as large a hole as possible should be dug. A pickaxe is more effective than a fork; alternatively, a pneumatic drill can be hired for the operation. In this way, any lime-tolerant tree can be grown anywhere. A handful of bonemeal or blood, fish and bone mixed in the soil and compost helps the long-term structure of the tree.

Having planted the tree, gently tread the soil, creating a saucer-shaped depression to help retain moisture. If the tree is only about 1m high it may not need staking. About 2m high and, if it will be rocked by wind, staking is essential. Get a wooden stake and a rubber tree band and attach the band low down, about 0.5m from the ground. The tree should bend with the wind so that its roots can reach down in resistance to it. Too much staking for too long inhibits good root growth and turns the tree into a cripple. Check the band after nine months, making sure that it is not too tight for the growing circumference of the tree, and, if it is, ease it out. A tree band which is left too tight can stifle the tree and impede its growth. After two or three years stakes should be removed.

Rabbits are all too often a problem, and if the entire circumference of the trunk is gnawed the tree may die. Spiral tree guards give effective protection. Deer too are a problem in many areas, and the best hope is to place a cylinder of wire, about 1m in diameter and 1.5m high, around the tree.

More garden trees, apparently three out of four, die during their first two years through a lack of moisture than for any other reason; all trees once planted must be watered during dry conditions until they are established. To reach the roots, it is better to water with three buckets every third day rather than one bucket every day. A hose, if not banned by local authorities, is even better.

When a mature tree, particularly a shallow-rooting crab or cherry, is showing signs of stress, turning on the hose for several hours – if permitted – can work wonders.

If a tree develops signs of chlorosis in its early years a dose of Sequestrene or some other iron compound can help. This should not be necessary indefinitely; some trees resist high alkalinity when young but on maturing overcome their initial reluctance.

CHAPTER 3

Shrubs

There is as yet no society called 'Men of Shrubs'. We wax lyrical about trees and marvel how the sap is drawn over a hundred feet to the sky, but shrubs have less powerful connotations. The word is derived from the Old English *scrybb*, related to the Low German *shrubben* meaning coarse, uneven, and the very sound associates with scrub and scruff. Victorian houses named 'The Shrubbery' induce visions of dusty evergreens, and grown randomly, shrubs can look like ill-assorted blobs. However, grown and placed with consideration they contour the garden, creating spaces. Many are stunningly beautiful. Others are a foil to bright colours or simply a rest from gaudiness. When herbaceous plants die down, the shape of shrubs becomes important. Holly can be grown for its berries or foliage but also clipped into architectural shapes. So can bay, box, yew, hawthorn and the shrubby *Lonicera nitida* 'Baggesen's Gold'. Spheres or cones of box can give structure. Vast numbers of shrubs, their roots not so demanding of depth, are tolerant of thin alkaline soils.

Many of the larger shrubs, including cotoneasters such as *C. × watereri*, tamarisk, *Photinia davidiana* and the lovely *Xanthoceras sorbifolium*, if placed centre stage look more shapely if their skirts are cut 0.5m from the ground to show a leg or two. In a small garden they can be grown as standards, giving height in an area where trees are impractical. In this way, too, spring bulbs can be planted under them.

OPPOSITE PAGE:
Cornus kousa *var.* chinensis.

SHRUBS FOR WINTER

Two hundred years ago, when the treasure stores of western China had yet to be broached, few winter-flowering shrubs were known. Today we can enjoy hardy, winter-flowering shrubs for months. In the cold their metabolism is slow and their need to attract the infrequent insect means that they flower longer than the weeks or days of most summer blooms.

Since they bloom in months of little light, they can usually take a shady spot. Many are fragrant and should be planted by the door. We wander less in the garden during winter, and a blast of fragrance when entering a house delights the spirit and is pure aromatherapy.

Christmas box, *Sarcococca humilis*, is so invaluable that no garden should be without it. Low, reaching about 1m after several years, evergreen with neat, small, glossy leaves, in February its scent bemuses, coming from white flowers so modest it is hard to locate the source. It needs no pruning. In the summer it bears red berries which turn black and persist with the flowers the following year. It takes shade, and does not object to being later smothered by showy summer flowers. Little seedlings can often be found growing under it. Rather taller and pinker but as fragrant is *S. hookeriana* var. *digyna*.

Mahonia, mostly from North America, is hardy, evergreen, interestingly but not dangerously spiky. All species are happy on alkaline soils and can take shade. Upright, with flowers like posies of yellow lily-of-the-valley in November and December, *Mahonia × media* 'Charity' reaches to about 3m or more, but, if it gets too tall, it can be cut back in spring, showing its yellow sap and wood. It may look drastic, but it will grow multi-branched from the cut stem and flower the following winter. Two

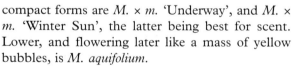

Mahonia × media *'Charity' in January.*

Cornus alba *'Sibirica' in January.*

compact forms are *M.* × *m.* 'Underway', and *M.* × *m.* 'Winter Sun', the latter being best for scent. Lower, and flowering later like a mass of yellow bubbles, is *M. aquifolium.*

Winter honeysuckle, *Lonicera fragrantissima*, has a stronger fragrance than *Mahonia* and is deciduous, flowering bare-stemmed in January and February. *L.* × *purpusii* is slightly more vigorous but produces fewer flowers. It should be cut back in spring when it has finished flowering, and, since it is not that attractive in the summer, merely a shrub covered in green leaves, it is best not planted in a focal point but beside another shrub which shows its glory later in the year.

Two viburnums are at their best in winter. Laurestinus, *Viburnum tinus*, from the Mediterranean has been in our gardens for centuries, and, being evergreen, needs careful siting because in the wrong place it looks lumpy. It is good in a corner, clipped back as a wall shrub, and can even be grown as a standard giving a vertical dimension to a small garden. Some varieties have dirty pink flowers, but the best is *V. t.* 'Gwenllian', pink in bud and opening white with a pink tinge, and *V. t.* 'French White'.

Viburnum × *bodnantense* at first glance hardly seems the same genus as laurestinus. It loses its leaves in winter and has little, deep pink buds, paler on opening, which have the most heavenly scent imaginable. The open flowers get browned by severe frosts, but then more buds open. *V.* × *b.* 'Dawn' is an excellent clone, with more and larger flowers, and *V.* × *b.* 'Deben's flowers are white.

The cornelian cherry, *Cornus mas*, is a large shrub with small, yellow flowers on bare stems, and later produces red, edible fruit. Wintersweet, *Chimonanthus praecox*, is excellent on alkaline soils, producing its scented, waxy, yellow flowers with purple anthers in later winter. If grown as a wall shrub, it will flower earlier. These are medium- to large-sized shrubs, but not to be forgotten is a very small one for a dry, sheltered, sunny place, *Coronilla glauca* 'Citrina', with greyish leaves and soft, yellow flowers wafting scent for weeks in late winter.

Daphne bholua 'Jacqueline Postill', the earliest flowering and not always the easiest *Daphne*, must have a deep topsoil which never dries out, but is worth trying for its wonderfully scented flowers, pink with a red reverse, in February.

In the dark months stems and leaves unregarded earlier among a mass of flowers suddenly spring to attention. Dogwoods such as *Cornus alba* 'Sibirica' have brilliant red stems particularly noticeable in the dormant months. The youngest stems give the brightest effect, and, although they can be stooled in February, it is better to cut back some of the older stems selectively in spring, so that they go on looking attractive until clothed by spring leaves. The white-stemmed bramble, *Rubus cockburnianus*, is often planted for the winter effect of its white stems, which from a distance look like a pale mauve haze, especially lovely in winter with the black leaves of the lily turf, *Ophiopogon planiscapus*, planted below. But, trouble is round the corner: this bramble can sucker like fury and is best grown in the confines of a buried container.

SHRUBS FOR LEAVES

The charm of several shrubs lies in their leaves and habit, providing a quiet counterfoil to brighter colours nearby. Variegated shrubs must be chosen with care, because, unless the variegation is precise and clear, with good colour and not a sickly merging green and yellow, they can look diseased and chlorotic. Perhaps the most beautiful of all variegated shrubs is the wedding cake tree, *Cornus controversa* 'Variegata', with fine green and white leaves hanging in tiers. In spring, when the leaf buds are just bursting, they almost look like flowers. It can take a purple clematis weaving through it. Although it needs no pruning, after fifteen years or so twigs between the tiers may need to be removed to keep the architectural structure. The plain green *Cornus controversa*, larger than the shrub, makes an attractive, small flowering tree.

The snowberry, *Symphoricarpus*, will grow anywhere, but it can be a pest, sending up suckers all over the place, with its only pleasure white bobbles

Cornus controversa
*'Variegata', coming
into leaf in April.*

Cornus controversa *'Variegata', the wedding cake tree, in flower.*

in autumn. Nicer and better behaved is a variegated snowberry, green and gold, *S. orbiculatus* 'Foliis Variegatus', rather smaller. Nearly all variegated plants, forming less chlorophyll, are not as vigorous as their green forms. Another attractive variegated shrub, rather larger and growing to 4m is the buckthorn, *Rhamnus alaternus* 'Argenteovariegata'. It can take a shady spot, it does not need pruning and can be useful as cutting foliage.

Euonymous comes in many guises, and *E. fortunei* 'Emerald 'n' Gold', despite its crass name, and its lovely sister *E. f.* 'Silver Queen', make attractive, low, variegated and evergreen shrubs, virtually ground cover, which, once established, can take dry soil in shade. Really cold weather gives the leaves a pinkish tinge. *Osmanthus heterophyllus* is often mistaken for holly but its leaves are paired in opposites rather than being alternate, giving it that neat precision of all shrubs with a similar leaf conjunction. It is a classy, evergreen shrub with fine marbled variegation that can take shade.

Holly, *Ilex aquifolium*, is a good-looking creature throughout the year and can take any aspect, although more berries will be produced in sun. The berries are borne on female plants and need a male nearby for pollination. The variegated *Ilex aquifolium* 'Argentea Marginata' is usually sold as a female, but if berries are wanted it is worth checking when buying. Curiously, two other variegated hollies named *I. a.* 'Golden Queen' and *I. a.* 'Silver Queen' are male. There is also the splendid hedgehog holly, *I. a.* 'Ferox Argentea' in its variegated form, with a mass of lacerating prickles along the leaf surface.

Shrubs or trees with silver, red or gold leaves make ideal gifts on wedding anniversaries when a couple have everything else they need. For ruby weddings, *Cercis canadensis* 'Forest Pansy' is a medium-sized shrub, easy to grow, with red, heart-shaped leaves. It should be planted in the west, where, for half an hour, the sinking sun glows through the leaves like stained glass. The smoke bush *Cotinus* 'Royal Purple' has a mass of maroon leaves with a haze of airy panicles whose effect lasts for weeks.

The red leaves of *Photinia* × *fraseri* 'Red Robin' emerge in spring, contrasting with the older, glossy, evergreen leaves and the effect can be startling. Although happy on alkaline soils, if the emerging leaves are dull or too liver-coloured, a dose of Sequestrene or another chelated iron compound will improve the colour the following year. In a good year it billows with lacy, white flowers. More refined and taller is *P. davidiana* with small, white flowers, attractive to bees and with some red leaves. Its plus is autumn berries.

ABOVE: *Leaf of* Cercis canadensis *'Forest Pansy', with the sun behind it.*

RIGHT: Cercis canadensis *'Forest Pansy' in its second year; in due course it becomes an attractive shrub, sometimes bearing pink flowers in May.*

The purple smoke bush, Cotinus *'Royal Purple', with* Clematis *'Mrs Cholmondeley' weaving through.*

Photinia × fraseri
'Red Robin', in flower.

Spiraea japonica 'Gold Flame' is small, easy and popular, and for some weeks in spring and early summer is striking with gold leaves tipped rose pink. Later, as it flowers, it relaxes into green mode. It can take any situation and a dry soil. The common elder, *Sambucus nigra*, despite the handiness of its flowers for cordials and champagnes, is not welcome but it does have some excellent relatives. *S. racemosa* 'Plumosa Aurea' has cut gold leaves, *S. nigra* 'Black Beauty' has purple leaves and dark pink flowers, and best of all is *S. n.* 'Black Lace', with serrated, wine-dark leaves framing stained pink flowers. These elders will take any situation, and, once established, they need regular pruning, with about three or more of the oldest stems being cut back in winter to ground level.

Colours appear differently according to the context they are seen in, and purple-leaved plants beside green can make the latter seem golden. *Berberis thunbergii* 'Atropurpurea Superba', impossibly prickly like all the berberis, can perform this function beside a green-leaved, flowering currant, and in autumn turns a fiery orange-red, with glossy little berries. *B. t.* 'Harlequin' has marbled, red leaves, and is very easy going. The occasional stem should be pruned to ground level to encourage new

growth, but if this is forgotten and the plant becomes tired and woody, the whole plant can be cut to the ground where it should rejuvenate after two years or so. If this seems too drastic, cut it back by a third one year, and another third the next.

The golden-leaved philadelphus, *P. coronarius* 'Aureus' is a beautiful lime gold for months, but in bright sun its leaves get scorched and its flowers are never produced in great profusion. Other good shrubs with golden leaves, handy for a contrast, a background or a golden anniversary present, are *Choisya ternata* 'Sundance', which, being evergreen, is particularly useful, *Ribes sanguineum* 'Brocklebankii' – again, take care lest the leaves get scorched by too much sun – and *Berberis thunbergii* 'Aurea'. None of these gold-leaved shrubs grows as large as its green counterparts.

Stag's horn sumach, *Rhus typhina*, is invasive, but a variety like the cut-leaved *R. t.* 'Dissecta' is worth growing for its velvet horns and ferny leaves, orange in autumn, but, like its parent, it does produce runners trying to elbow the neighbours aside. These must be torn out, unless it is given a glade of its own.

The long-veined banners of *Phormium tenax* are green, purple or multi-coloured. From a distance they look like a huge crown and close to they look as if cut from some superior handmilled paper. Phormi-um can be grown in a mixed border or with other shrubs to add varied colour and texture. It needs a sheltered, sunny spot, and the multi-coloured varieties such as *P. t.* 'Dazzler' are less hardy than the purple and basic green type.

Adam's needle, *Yucca filamentosa*, and the larger *Y. gloriosa* in a sheltered position produce flowers like frozen fountains and their displays of sword leaves gives them an architectural presence throughout the year. *Y. gloriosa* can take some winter shade as long as it is sheltered and in well-drained soil, but these are essentially sun-loving plants, best not too near a path in case their vicious leaves spike passers-by.

For a confined space, *Pittosporum tenuifolium* 'Purpureum' is excellent, with glossy, little leaves which open pale green and turn dark maroon. In winter it looks lively with *Iris unguicularis* nearby, or in summer contrasting with gold and green shrubs. It needs to be out of harsh winds and requires no pruning, but, if desired, it will respond to a trim. Another shrub needing a sheltered site, this time in the shade, is *Fatsia japonica*, with its palm hands; it can take alkalinity, but the richer the soil the larger the leaves become.

SHRUBS FOR SPRING AND SUMMER

Shrubs with Scented Flowers

On the thinnest alkaline soils some shrubs flourish, relishing stony dryness, and many are scented. They are sun lovers, often aromatic, grey leaved and with their pastel flower colours give the garden a feel of the Mediterranean, where they often come from. Some are herbs which have been grown for centuries.

The hardiest and easiest lavender and the one with the sweetest smell is old English lavender – in fact, only wild in Spain, France, Italy and Greece – *Lavandula angustifolia*. Beautiful, deep purple-blue varieties, not too tall, are *L. a.* 'Hidcote' and *L. a.* 'Twickel Purple'. If left unpruned it gets tired, bare and leggy. To keep it in a state of prolonged juvenility cut each stem back after flowering to where next year's growth can be seen as little white bumps. Cutting lower into old wood will be murder. French

Yucca gloriosa.

lavender, *L. stoechas*, is not so tough nor long-living and its scent has a hospital whiff of camphor, but is a lovely thing with its bracts erect like rabbits' ears. Other lavenders such as cut-leaved although delightful are not totally hardy.

Rosemary from the Mediterranean is more than happy basking in sun on thin alkaline soils. It is amenable and can be grown as a low hedge, often sending out runners. With support it can be trained as a standard and even pinned back as a wall shrub. The flowers of the basic *Rosmarinus officinalis* are palest blue, but lovelier is *R. o.* 'Severn Sea', the deepest sky. Like lavender, it resents harsh pruning and will not sprout from old wood.

Russian sage, *Perovskia atriplicifolia* 'Blue Spire', with its silver, mint-scented leaves is similar in its

Rosemary grown as a wall shrub; it is amenable to training as a wall shrub or standard.

ladanifer, with white, crumpled tissue flowers, chocolate blotches at the centre around stamens like gold filings, and its scent coming from the sticky, aromatic foliage. The flowers do not last long, but bloom intermittently through the summer. As a shrub, it is not long-living, but cutting back gently in late spring helps new growth and a longer life. It enjoys the poorest soil, the dryer and sunnier the better.

Many substantial shrubs are happy on alkaline soils but do appreciate rich planting with plenty of compost and a handful of bonemeal. The viburnum for scent is *V. carlesii*, with the most gorgeous fragrance imaginable and its blossom a mass of white flowers and pink buds. It is often sold grafted to the root of *V. lantana*, the wild viburnum, and an eye needs to be kept open for alien suckers which may take over. *V. × burkwoodii* 'Anne Russell', equally fragrant, is a pure white species. They are both over all too soon.

With an equally wonderful scent is *Daphne odora*, and here for once the variegated form, *D.o.* 'Aureomarginata' with a white pencil line round the leaves, is if anything more vigorous than the parent plant. It performs best out of full sun. Flowering rather later but with as good a scent is *D. × burkwoodii* with pink flowers and covered by bees. No pruning of *Daphne* should be necessary. Oddly, although *D. mezereum* is a chalk native – and worth growing – as a genus not all daphnes are that happy in alkaline soil, some preferring a richer, more neutral loam.

The flowering currant, *Ribes sanguineum*, in both leaf and flower has the rich, musty smell of blackcurrants, which some love and others find stifling. Soft red forms like *R. s.* 'Pulborough Scarlet' are stunning, but murky pink varieties are grown too often, sometimes making an awkward contrast with bright daffodils below. Try growing *R. s.* 'Tydeman's White', with long racemes but about two-thirds the usual height, with white Mount Hood daffodils in front. The shades of cream and white are beautiful. The clove currant, *R. odoratum*, bears golden, scented flowers in spring.

No self-respecting Victorian garden could be without a lilac, and their thick mounds of blossom exuding wafts of some expensive soap are spectacular in early summer. There are good cultivars such as *Syringa vulgaris* 'Souvenir de Louis Spaeth', purple, and *S. v.* 'Primrose', cream. Flowering is

demands, needing full sun and an open soil. Its little, blue flowers bloom for weeks in late summer and early autumn, producing a smoky blue haze. It may be safely cut to the ground in spring, and new shoots will soon appear.

The little Australian mint bush, *Prostanthera rotundifolia*, has aromatic, evergreen leaves and whitish flowers in early summer, and, although reputed to be tender, will survive frosty winters against a south-facing wall in a well-drained soil. Myrtle, flowering later, is rather similar in looks and habits, and the small-leaved variety *Myrtus communis* subsp. *tarentina* is hardier than the common type.

There are many varieties of cistus from southern France, Spain and Morocco, white and shades of pink, and one of the most beautiful is *Cistus*

increased if the old seedheads are removed. If necessary, it can be cut back, but it really needs plenty of space to flourish and it is not that interesting for the rest of the year, although climbers such as clematis can give it later excitement. An alternative is a smaller species, for instance, Korean lilac, *S. velutina*, a slow-growing species with very dainty flowers, or the Persian lilac, *S.* × *persica*.

Mexican orange blossom, *Choisya ternata*, related to citrus and with similar flowers and leaves which when rubbed exude a pungent smell, distinct from that of the flowers, is lovely with its evergreen leaves and early white blossom, but in a frost pocket it can come into blossom too soon and get blasted. But then, it usually flowers in late summer. If it is getting out of hand, every fourth year it can be cut back to within 0.5m of ground level, to produce fresh glossy growth and eventually flower again. Also with aromatic leaves, the all spice, *Calycanthus floridus* is a little shrub endearing itself to those who enjoy the quirky. Its leaves and curious dull red flowers have a strong spicy scent.

Osmanthus delavayi is neat, evergreen, with small flowers and a good scent in early summer. Similar, but flowering in late summer, is *Abelia grandiflora*, with scented white flowers held in pink calyces which persist and look like tiny flowers themselves when the blooms have fallen.

In high summer nothing compares with the pervading scent of *Philadelphus*, full, sweet and with a hint – as perfumiers say are nearly all the sexiest scents – of the faecal. *Philadelphus* is at home on alkaline soils in all its guises, from *P.* 'Beauclerk', single white flowers with pinkish centres, for large gardens, and the little, double white *P.* 'Manteau d'Hermine', for small ones. Its only problem is a tendency to harbour blackfly; these can be rubbed or pinched out, or removed for the season with a blast of insecticide.

Everyone knows the butterfly bush, *Buddleja davidii*, crammed with successive swarms of invading butterflies in August. If it has a chance, it will self-seed. One of the loveliest varieties is *B. d.* 'Dark Knight', and this and the white varieties are just as attractive to butterflies. It can be pruned in winter to within a few centimetres of the ground, but since not everyone wants the stumps that result from hard pruning and the fact is that it will still flower without pruning, it can be left until it gets woody and

out of hand and then cut severely back every five years or so. *B. globosa* bears yellow balls, interesting but not so beautiful as the common buddleia. *B. alternifolia* blooms earlier and is graceful with flowers along its arching stems, but to do well it needs space and a deeper topsoil than the common buddleia.

Colletia hystrix is a ferocious beast covered with frothy, white, scented flowers in summer, and, if you bend to sniff, it spits like a cat with outstretched claws. It does well on poor soils and if caged in a corner becomes a handsome and unusual garden ornament. Another spiky little number with cream, scented flowers is *Poncirus trifoliata*, the Japanese bitter orange, luring insects but repelling any attempt to touch it.

Spanish broom, *Spartium junceum*, is not for those who like their yellows soft and faded; its gold pea blooms are bright with a vengeance. It has a head-turning scent, it likes sun and an open situation, and flowers during late summer into autumn. It can be trained single-stemmed as a small tree.

Shrubs for Flowers

Virtually all flowers have some smell, even if it is not intense or sweet, and learning them is a question of slow exploration, breathing in one flower after another, never more than two or three at a time. These include shrubs grown for the glamour of their flowers rather than their faint, exiguous fragrance. One is *Viburnum plicatum* 'Mariesii', which, for a while in the right spot, becomes a star with huge, white bracts of flowers falling in tiers. Rather taller is the snowball tree, *V. opulus* 'Sterile', dotted in early summer with spherical panicles of flowers, and its counterpart the guelder rose, *V. opulus*, with lace-cap flowers and fruit in autumn. All are reliable, will grow anywhere and briefly lighten a dark background. Performing the same function later in the year is *Hydrangea paniculata* 'Grandiflora', with mounds of creamy white flowers. Most hydrangeas, unlike the viburnums, are essentially acid lovers, but tolerate alkalinity as long as they are in moist soil and out of full sun. Their roots must never dry out. The flowers of *H. macrophylla* turn out a perfectly passable pink and need a colorant to become blue.

The elegant *Cornus kousa* var. *chinensis* is often cited as a calcifuge, but although it is similar to the

American *C. florida*, a flowering dogwood usually unsuccessful on alkaline soils, this comes from China and, provided it is well planted, grows into a most attractive shrub on dry chalky soil with white bracts turning pink, followed by little strawberry fruits. Often, Chinese plants of the same genus are happier with alkalinity than their American or Japanese counterparts. This one prefers light shade, and is one of these amenable shrubs that need no pruning.

Forsythia is one of those plants, like pampas grass, which will flourish anywhere and each spring the partnership of bright yellow forsythia and sugar-pink cherry blossom appears in hundreds of gardens. If this jars, try growing the weeping variety *Forsythia suspensa* 'Nymans', with pendulous sprays of pale primrose flowers.

Xanthoceras sorbifolium is one of those plants hovering between the categories of tree and shrub and can be grown as a rounded mass or trained as a standard to give height in a small garden. It has attractive pinnate leaves and in spring white flowers with carmine eyes. After a warm summer it produces conker-like seed pods, rather like tops, much enjoyed by children.

Three excellent medium to large shrubs are the beauty bush *Deutzia gracilis* and *Weigelia florida* with reliable attractive blooms in early summer, and *Kolkwitzia amabilis* 'Pink Cloud', also called the beauty bush showing a mass of deep pink flowers with orange throats on slightly arching stems. There are several varieties of *Deutzia*, growing eventually to about 2m, and the ones with white blossom, each flower with a little inner skirt, are some of the best. Smaller varieties are *D. corymbosa*, which reaches to less than 1m, *D. gracilis* and *D. pulchra*. The flowers of *Weigela florida* are a touch less refined, and range from yellow and white to pink and red. *W. f.* 'Alexandra' has scarlet flowers looking dramatic with dark red leaves, and *W. f.* 'Pink Poppet' is handy as a dwarf.

Rubus is another easygoing floriferous shrub for early summer, this time with white blooms, and *R.* 'Benenden' has the largest blooms of all. *Kerria japonica* 'Pleniflora' with its double button flowers settles happily on poor, alkaline soils, sending up suckers everywhere. In a confined space this may be a nuisance, but the faults of any plant can be a blessing in a different situation, and *Kerria* is a handy shrub where dense cover is required. Flowering at the same time are *Spiraea* 'Arguta', a mass of delicate white blossom on bending stems in May, and the one *Exochorda* which can settle into an alkaline soil, *E. korolkowii*. Both these last two are exquisite, white-blossomed shrubs for a small garden.

Viburnum plicatum *'Mariesii', with a golden, variegated euonymus.*

Magnolias are at their best on acid soils, but, given a decent depth of alkaline topsoil they make a respectable showing for a number of years, if not indefinitely. The best is *Magnolia* × *loebneri* 'Leonard Messel', a hybrid between *M. kobus*, happy on alkaline soils but taking eight years to flower, and *M. stellata*. *M.* × *l.* 'Leonard Messel' flowers straight away, with pale pink strap petals fading to white stars. It looks brilliant against a dark background. *M. grandiflora*, with huge white flowers in August can also take alkalinity, but is better grown as a sheltered wall shrub rather than a standard in all but the mildest situations.

Evergreen *Ceanothus*, from California, is stunning in late spring with its clouds of blossom, deepest blue, the colour of distance, mountains and sky. It is not long-living but worth growing for ten seasons or so of beauty. In the milder situation of the coast or a city garden *C. arboreus* can be grown as a small tree, while in frostier regions evergreen species such as *C.* 'Puget Blue' are best against a south- or west-facing wall. In a particularly cold area with late frosts it is best to plant a hardier deciduous variety such as *C.* 'Gloire de Versailles' which flowers later.

Tamarisk is best known in coastal gardens, where its bending sprays of tiny pink flowers toss in sea winds, but, in fact, it is hardy and, enjoying any well-drained soil, it is more than happy in most limy areas. It can get rather straggly after a few years, in which case if it is a variety such as *Tamarix tetrandra*, flowering on the previous year's growth, it can be cut back hard after flowering, or, if flowering like *T. ramosissima* 'Pink Cascade' on the current season's growth, it can be cut back in February. It can be grown as a hedge and also looks graceful grown as a standard, with the lower branches and any suckers having been removed. A mild day in winter is the time for such an operation.

Tree peonies, *Paeonia suffruticosa*, may look stumpy in winter but in the growing season the leaves look as if cut by scissors and in early June the flowers come on like dancers at the Folies Bergères, all frothy skirts and lace knickers. They grow to about 1.5m, and for glamour they are incomparable – as well as being hardy and reliable – with as few troubles as their herbaceous counterparts, although they may slightly stoop with age. Two glorious varieties are *P. s.* 'Nigata Akashigata', with

Ceanothus.

blush petals with magenta strips leading to a boss of gold stamens, and *P.* × *lemoinei* 'Souvenir de Maxine Cornu', a welter of gold and orange. Taller, handsome and more restrained is the yellow tree peony, *P. lutea* var. 'Ludlowii', which keeps its upright stance into old age. Almost no pruning is required, although three older stems can be removed in the spring to encourage fresh growth.

The pea family includes a vast number of shrubs, all demanding a sunny spot, some picky about their soil and others tolerating what they are given. The easygoing *Piptanthus nepalensis* has a mass of golden flowers in June, followed by green, translucent pods showing rows of seeds. It requires virtually no pruning, apart from the excising of dead stems, and lives for years. *Genista aetnensis*, with yellow flowers, can take a thin soil and provides a bamboo-like screen about 2m high, giving an intriguing effect when half the garden is seen through it. Bladder senna, *Colutea arborescens*, has pleasant, ferny foliage and pale yellow flowers which become curious puffy seed pods, and is also happy on thin alkaline soil. The brooms, usually seen on more acid soils, are attractive but not long-lived; this can be a bonus when they are used in exposed situations as nurse shrubs to shelter a newly planted tree which will eventually outgrow and outlive them. The spreading broom *Cytisus × kewensis* is a rich cream colour in spring and needs very little pruning.

Hypericum calycinum, with its shining yellow flowers, is given a bad name because of its invasive habit, but every vice may become a virtue and in a larger garden this can be a perfect ground cover. For a smaller garden *H.* 'Hidcote' is invaluable, with its large flowers carrying on for months, and so is *H. × moserianum* with golden flowers cupping red anthers from early summer to late autumn. *Hypericum* can take full sun but ideally prefers light shade.

No small, dry garden should be without *Potentilla*, with its succession of flowers in yellow, white or orange through the summer. It revels in full sun. *P. fruticosa* 'Abbotswood', with pure white flowers and grey-green leaves, forms a low mound. Excellent too are *P. f.* 'Tilford Cream', and *P. f.* 'Red Ace'. *Helianthemum*, rock roses, are also classics for alkaline gardens with their little mounds of flowers in a profusion of colours – white, pinks, reds, apricots and yellows. The infertile double varieties flower much longer than the singles with only five petals. A light trim in spring reinvigorates and ensures a continued display of flowers.

The sun-loving *Hebes* are tidy plants with their neat pattern of growth, pairs of shining opposite leaves sprouting at right angle to the next pair. Unfortunately, the drabber colours tend to be hardier than the richer hued varieties, which may be wiped out in a severe winter. Hebes require a very light prune in spring to keep them neat. *Hebe pinguifolia* 'Pagei' has white flowers on a carpet of grey leaves, and *H. albicans* 'Autumn Glory' is taller, with gorgeous purple flowers until the autumn.

The hardy fuchsias will grace a shady spot in late summer. *Fuchsia magellanica* has long red and purple flowers and is particularly elegant, while the white *F. m.* 'Alba' or the palest pink *F. m.* 'Hawkcrest' look like drops of water against a dark background. They can be cut back in the winter.

For a sunny position in late summer two excellent, small, blue-flowered plants will enliven the scene. *Caryopteris × clandonensis* 'Arthur Simmonds', which is also known as blue spiraea, has tufts of misty blue flowers appearing at the axils of aromatic leaves. It is reliable and a lover of alkaline soils. *Ceratostigma willmottianum*, a hardy member of the plumbago family, needs a richer soil to achieve its stunning blue flowers which carry on until the autumn frosts, but it has no objection to alkalinity as such.

Tree mallow, Lavatera, *in a border edged with cotton lavender.*

The tree mallow is not long-lived, rarely lasting more than a few years, but it is a splendid sight in later summer. In a single season a small plant can grow into a grand shrub packed with flowers, which may be white, pink or darkest wine. The well-known *Lavatera × clementii* 'Barnsley' is palest pink with a dark eye, but has a tendency to revert to plain pink. These mallows cannot take a harsh winter, and, for insurance, cuttings are easily taken in early summer. A light soil and full sun are essential for successful flowering and, to help prolong its life, cut each shoot back by a third in the autumn and in the following spring cut back to a few buds.

SHRUBS FOR AUTUMN

Wandering along downland hedgerows in autumn, among the hips and haws, are the berries of *Euonymus europaeus*, an improbably exotic confection of orange casings holding bright pink berries. Earlier, the flowers are barely noticeable. For leaf colouring, grow *E. alatus*, with winged stems where in a sunny location it turns the deepest red. On highly alkaline soil the red may not be so intense.

Both the green and the purple variety of the smoke bush, *Cotinus*, turn orange during the first frosts, the best variety for autumn being *C.* 'Flame', its leaves becoming a rich marmalade. *Berberis* has good autumn colour, and one of the best is *B. thunbergii* 'Red Chief', with red leaves and prickly stems bearing delicate berries like oval coral beads.

There are numerous species of cotoneaster, the little white flowers attracting insects in summer and becoming in autumn a mass of berries which persist. *Cotoneaster × watereri* is upright, the size of a small tree, holding its branches and berries horizontally, rather like a miniature cedar of Lebanon. With judicious pruning, leaving only three or four bare stems at the base, it makes a satisfying focal point. *C. dammeri* is low and spreading.

Many wild roses have spectacular autumn hips and some of the best are the scarlet flagons of *Rosa moyesei*, the glossy beads of *R. glauca* and the tomato hips of *R. rugosa*.

Cotoneaster × watereri *in winter.*

Leycesteria formosa is a useful, second-division shrub, over 1m high, easygoing, bearing a mass of pink bracts with white flowers, and later large, purple berries, like exotic, dangling earrings.

SHRUBS FOR SCREENING

A pylon, a hideous shed or building, or a need for privacy all call for screening, and the best plants for this are evergreen. Gale-force winds call for screening too, and here a group or plants or a hedge is better than any wall because it can absorb some of the impact so that the wind does not sweep over and create greater turbulence beyond.

Some of the best evergreen shrubs are the laurels, a term which includes bay, the true laurel, *Laurus nobilis* from Greece and Turkey where it turns mountainsides in May into scented gardens. Laurel also includes the cherry laurel and the Portuguese laurel, *Prunus laurocerasus* and *P. lusitanica*, the spurge laurel *Daphne laureola* (not so brilliant

on thin chalk soils), *Viburnum tinus* and the spotted laurel, *Aucuba japonica* 'Crotonifolia', most of which will do the job of screening on alkaline soils. Some have caused poisoning by being used in cooking instead of bay. For screening, the cherry laurel is quick and effective, but on poor soils Portuguese laurel is a better bet. *Viburnum tinus* has the plus of winter flowers.

Photinia × *fraseri* 'Red Robin' and *P. davidiana* have red leaves among the green, and, like *Elaeagnus ebbingei* 'Gilt Edge', a variegated evergreen, are useful for blocking unwanted sights. The holm oak, *Quercus ilex*, will grow to tree size and for a high screen can be invaluable, particularly beside the sea where it is not affected by salt winds.

All of these shrubs can be left free-standing or trimmed. In the latter case they look better if they are cut with secateurs so that the large glossy leaves are not left torn and browning; however, this may be the straw that breaks the camel's back and a hedge trimmer can be used to give a moderately decent result.

If bay has got out of hand, it will not resent hard clipping in April, when a shaggy monster can be turned into a huge topiary egg or drum within an hour.

Sea buckthorn, *Hippophae rhamnoides*, can make a good windbreak, and if female plants are grown with one or two males for pollination, will have a mass of orange berries in late summer. If it is too happy, it can send out invasive suckers. Hazel will quickly grow into a screen, and a golden variety is *Corylus avellana* 'Aurea'.

Bamboo rustling in the wind can lessen the sound of traffic as well screening it from view. Once established, canes can be cut to support runner beans or bent into ovals for container plants to grow up. *Fargesia murielae* grows into a dense mass of slim canes – technically culms – with lots of small, bright leaves. Golden bamboo, *Phyllostachys aureosulcata* 'Spectabilis', is a larger, stately plant with enough energy to cope in poorer soils, and looks dramatic with its mass of golden rods in winter. Incorporate plenty of compost when planting it.

Clipped bay, Laurus nobilis.

Phyllostachys aureocaulis *'Spectabilis', golden bamboo.*

PLANTING

All shrubs should be planted like trees, in a hole at least twice the size of the roots and filled with good things like compost and a handful of bonemeal or fish, blood and bone. If the hole is in solid chalk, hack the edges so that there is rubble at the base to give the roots a better chance to penetrate. If the shrub has a graft point, as with some *Viburnum* and tree peonies, make sure that this is just below the soil level. In dry soil stamp a depression around the newly planted shrub, so that in its early years any water does not run away. It will need watering while becoming established.

PRUNING

The individual pruning needs of some shrubs such as *Daphne* – rarely any ever – have been mentioned already. Generally speaking, the right time for pruning is after flowering or after the effect required. With plants flowering after midsummer, *Perovskia* and *Caryopteris*, for instance, this usually means waiting until they have got through the winter, and pruning on a mild day in early spring. When pruning a plant grown for its berries the time for action is early spring.

When it comes to pruning shrubs which flower before midsummer, the winter-flowering shrubs, as well as *Philadelphus*, *Kolkwitzia*, *Deutzia*, *Rubus*, *Ribes* and the like, the time for action is immediately after flowering.

Cut back three or four old stems to ground level to encourage further shoots, and trim back some of the longer stems. Take care not to give a topiarized effect with every shoot the same length – it looks unnatural and too tidy. Unless, of course, that is the effect required.

If a shrub has got totally out of hand, it can be cut almost to the ground on a mild winter's day, fed and trusted that, though it may not flower for a season, if established it will send out strong new shoots. However, not all shrubs may survive such drastic treatment. To be on the safe side, cut some of the stems to ground level and the rest a third of their length one year, and another third the next, until it is within the bounds required.

In some years life is too hectic to get around to any pruning, and most shrubs, in fact, will give a splendid performance for many seasons without any attention whatsoever. Considering their natural habit in the wild, this is not so surprising.

HEDGING

Why is yew the ideal hedging? Its dark green is the perfect backdrop for a spiraea or magnolia in bloom or the froth of herbaceous plants. Well cut, it looks satisfyingly green, crisp and geometric in winter. It grows on every soil including the thinnest alkaline. If neglected it can be renovated. It needs to be clipped only once a year to look as tight as wallpaper. It grows far faster than is popularly imagined. One possible disadvantage is that, being poisonous, the foliage could kill cattle in an adjoining field. Oddly, although the seeds too are lethal, the sweet and tasty flesh of the berries is not, and when berries are eaten by birds the seeds are later voided.

An alternative to yew, and burglar- and cattle-proof in eight years, is holly, *Ilex aquifolium*, making a handsome, glossy hedge. For berries, make sure female hollies are planted, bearing in mind that they will need at least one adjacent male holly for pollination.

Escallonia is another evergreen hedge, mostly happy in alkaline soils and, unlike holly, with no objection to maritime breezes on the coast. Some varieties are slightly tender but others such as *E.* 'Slieve Donard' are hardy enough to survive considerable cold inland. Privet, often seen in chalkland hedgerows, is frequently despised but the Victorians found it a wonderful standby, with its sweet, stuffy flowers in August and later black berries; well fed and cared for it makes a good-looking hedge. Golden privet, *Ligustrum ovalifolium* 'Aureum', makes beautiful hedging and can also be grown as a standard.

Coniferous hedges of the Leyland cypress, *Cupressocyparis leylandii* and the western red cedar, *Thuya plicata* grow quickly, a blessing at first and a curse later, but, well cared for and kept within bounds, they are handsome with a good tight finish, exuding a pleasant fruity scent when cut. In some cases it is appropriate to let them do their own thing; a line of untrimmed Leyland cypresses grows unchecked, garlanded by the rambling rose 'Kiftsgate' in a Kent garden bordering the M25 motorway, and marginally dampens the roar of traffic.

Sometimes a country garden makes a transition from formality and exotica near the house to rusticity in the countryside beyond, and here lines of evergreen hedging patrolling the outer boundaries appear harsh. Gentler, deciduous hedging is required. A beech hedge holds its leaves through the winter, and, when they fall in February, the bare stems are like a louvred screen, with glimpses of adjoining spaces. Hornbeam is the neatest deciduous hedge, naturally growing in a compact manner and taking any situation.

Flowering hedges include the most historic hedging of all, hawthorn or quick, *Crataegus laevigata*, spangled with white flowers in early May and best in a rustic setting. *Prunus cerasifera* 'Pissardii', bearing pale pink flowers in March, can be grown as a hedge, making a good and unusual dark background for herbaceous plants.

Within the garden, low informal hedging is often needed for defining spaces. Box, *Buxus sempervirens*, is another classic. Neat, evergreen, with a pleasant smell (which Queen Anne loathed), it is perfect for low hedging within the garden and around herbs or a rose garden. *B. s.* 'Latifolia Maculata' has yellow new growth and through it can be seen the darker, older leaves like shot taffeta. Dwarf box, *B. microphylla*, is prone to blight which shows in dead patches on the green. Hard clipping helps to avert the danger of attack.

Lavender, rosemary and fuchsia, cotoneaster, the snowberry and most shrubs can be planted as informal hedges. *Lonicera nitida* 'Baggesen's Gold' is low and evergreen, but grows at such a rate that it needs frequent clipping, at least three times a year, otherwise it becomes a mass of spikily uncontrolled spurs. Rugosa and other roses are often recommended for hedging, but they tend to be tall and leggy, and in winter on either side of a path are like barbed wire hemming in a prison walk.

Planting and Maintaining Hedging

A good hole, a decent dollop of compost or rotted manure and a handful of blood, fish and bone or bonemeal, as we have seen, speeds any shrub or hedge on its way. As with trees and shrubs, in shallow soils it is best to break down the chalk or limestone rubble so the roots have a chance to penetrate. A straight line rather than two lines with hedging plants staggered between is better, because

Ligustrum ovalifolium *'Aureum', variegated golden privet as standard in Yorkshire.*

a good hedge does not have to be thick. Aim to keep the base wider than the top, with a slight buttress slope on either side. This will allow the base to get sufficient sun, and prevent 'church windows' developing at the base. For the first two years keep the hedge watered during drier months. For this, a leaky hose can be invaluable.

It is said that Derby Day is the time to cut box and yew. In fact, at the National Trust garden of Hinton Ampner in Hampshire, where some of the finest box and yew hedges are grown, the hedges are cut three times a year to hold their tight finish. For those content with a single annual clipping, which gives a very decent effect, August or September is the month, when the yew is not yet dormant, the birds have finished nesting and the fledglings are flown. The fast-growing conifers such as the Leyland cypress and *Thuya plicata* will need two trimmings a year to be kept in line, in May and August.

When an existing garden is taken over, the problem all too often is a hedge that has got completely out of hand. With a neglected yew hedge, keep the top green, to encourage the rising sap. Then cut one side as far back as you want, and fresh greenery will sprout from the trunk itself. You can do one

ABOVE: *Yew cones and box hedging, contrasting with rough grass.*

BELOW: *Box spirals stand sentinel beside a gateway.*

side one year and the other the next. When the sides are sufficiently green, you can cut the top off. This same method applies to deciduous hedges, but the time for clipping or renovation here is February when the sap is about to rise.

CHAPTER 4

Climbers and Wall Shrubs

Climbers are for clothing breeze-block walls, garlanding brick, stone, cob and flint walls, trailing through trees and shrubs and extending seasonal colour. They are entrepreneurs, climbing on others' backs to reach the light. In the wild they claw, scramble and wriggle their way up, trailing over cliffs and festooning trees, shrubs and fallen logs. Where shrubs fail, their climbing counterparts often succeed – not all hydrangeas are at their best on alkaline soils, but *Hydrangea anomala* subsp. *petiolaris* covers a wall in minutes; a hybrid tea rose such as 'Mme Caroline Testout' may sit and sulk while 'Climbing Mme Caroline Testout' is ready and willing.

CLEMATIS

There are clematis blooming every month, from rosy *Clematis cirrhosa* 'Freckles', with its adorable red dusting, which, in a sheltered corner or in the soil of a cold greenhouse, can flower in December, to the little primrose-scented *C. rehderiana* which carries flowers from late September to November. The seedheads of several, for instance, *C. tangutica*, *C. orientalis* and *C. serratifolia*, glisten in the autumn light. In spring birds use faded seedheads to line their nests.

On poor, dry soil clematis may be subject to wilt, a fungal complaint which causes a splendidly growing plant suddenly to collapse and die. This can occur on east-facing walls which tend to be dryer, away from westerly rains. Here, the only hope is to cut the plant to the ground and to trust, if it has

been planted with some buds below soil level, that new shoots will emerge. If, with plenty of humus incorporated in the soil and plentiful watering, a clematis still wilts, it is probably one of the fussier, large-flowered hybrids. The clematis to plant in such conditions is one of the *C. viticella* cultivars which, as long as well planted, cope with aplomb in appalling conditions. The flowers may not be huge, but en masse they are stunning. Some of the best are: 'Mme Julia Correvon', lush, dark red; 'Polish Spirit', rich violet and flowering for weeks; 'Alba Luxurians', which starts flowering with green-edged, white petals (the technical name is tepals, since clematis do not have true petals held in a calyx) before producing pure white; and the most glamorous of the group, 'Venosa Violacea' with large, purple petals ribbed lacy white. Other good ones include 'Minuet'; pale blue 'Prince Charles'; 'Betty Corning' with palest blue bells; and 'Victor Hugo', purple-blue. They all flower after midsummer and are garden essentials.

Other small-flowered clematis, the species and near species, tend to be more tolerant of dryness than the large-flowered cultivars. In spring the little *C. alpina* with its single flowers and *C. macropetala* with its double flowers are showy, and one of the best of the former is blue 'Francis Rivis'. In a sheltered spot *C. armandii*, with its glossy evergreen leaves and vanilla-scented flowers does well against a wall, one of its best cultivars being *C. a.* 'Snowdrift'. When buying named cultivars of these or other clematis, it is important to get them from a reputable source because what can happen in street markets is that the clematis on offer is a seedling rather than a cutting, so, although sold under the name of its parent, the blue of the so-called *C. alpina* 'Francis Rivis' will not be as deep as the original, and the so called *C. armandii* 'Snowdrift' may

OPPOSITE PAGE:
Clematis *'Marie Boisselot'*.

Clematis armandii *'Snowdrift', a scented, evergreen clematis which can be rampant.*

Clematis serratifolia *above hips of* Rosa rugosa *in September.*

Clematis connata, *flowering in September.*

be scentless. Only with a cutting can you have all the qualities of the original plant. Many other plants, likewise, do not necessarily breed true.

C. montana goes on the rampage in late spring, clothing walls, smothering fences and spiralling along telephone wires. 'Marjorie' is a double variety with pale orange and white flowers which looks slightly khaki when the first buds open but later reveals its true colours. *C. m.* var. 'Grandiflora' is white, slightly scented and will flower on a north-facing wall, and *C. m. rubens* 'Tetrarose' is pink. *C. jouiniana* 'Praecox' is a late season hybrid between our native old man's beard and *C. heracleifolia* and will scramble up a support, producing a mass of pale blue flowers, a touch dull on their own but very pretty with another clematis, say 'Mme Julia Correvon' or a deep purple *C. jackmanii* hybrid, weaving through it. In August comes *C. tangutica*, so similar to the lemon-peel clematis *C. orientalis* – of which 'Bill Mackenzie' is a large, well hung variety – that one wonders why both are marketed. *C. serratifolia* with cut leaves and primrose petals is late flowering, and if planted at the base of a rugosa, about 1m from the main stem, this clematis will work its way through the host while the rose is flowering, then flower with pale gold petals contrasting with the red hips of the rugosa before turning into silky cocoons of seedheads. In autumn, or spring, the clematis is cut to 20cm from the ground and fed, leaving the host free.

Most of the species clematis can be persuaded to grow up trees and shrubs. 'Venosa Violacea' will grow up a hawthorn and, with a single-flowered variety like *Crataegus laevigata* 'Crimson Cloud', first there are the red hawthorn flowers, then the purple and white clematis among its branches, and in autumn the red polka dots of hawthorn berries. Evergreens are not happy hosts, and a bay tree particularly objects, developing dead patches under the shade of its guest. Deciduous trees and shrubs are preferable, particularly when they come into leaf and flower while the clematis is journeying through them.

For autumn scent, and a north-facing wall, the little, pale yellow bells of *C. rehderiana* are perfect, and continue for months. It is not a hit-you-in-the-eye clematis, but subtle. Even later, but not flowering for so long, is the unscented *C. connata* with its pale, neat bells.

Say 'clematis' and most people think of the large-flowered hybrids. With these, on alkaline and particularly on dryer soils it is best to go for the most floriferous. Utterly reliable, unfading in full sun, with a shower of blue flowers every year, is 'Perle d'Azur',

flowering after midsummer. 'Ernest Markham' is an excellent deep red, flowering in June but, when happy, both earlier and later. The staunch 'Comtesse de Bouchaud' is reliable and deep mauve-pink, with masses of flowers each July. 'John Huxtable' is a good, late, white clematis, flowering in August, but the most beautiful white clematis is 'Marie Boisselot', with clear white petals and light cream sepals, an eye-stopper every time. It flowers in May and again in later summer.

There are clematis, small-flowered species and large-flowered cultivars for every aspect, north, south, east and west. Most clematis specialists produce catalogues marking the preferred aspect of each variety.

Planting

All clematis should be watered thoroughly before planting, and, if pot-bound, the yellow roots slightly teased out. It must be planted in a hole at least twice and preferably several times larger than the size of the roots and filled with good things like compost and a handful of bonemeal. Good drainage is essential, and if the ground tends to sogginess in winter, a quantity of gravel at the base will help. Place the clematis with its supporting cane

Clematis *'Perle d'Azur'*.

tilting towards the wall or wires where it is to grow. Plant with the first pair of buds buried in the soil. This will ensure that, if damaged by scratching chickens or digging dogs or succumbing to wilt, the buried buds will send new shoots and allow its survival. In dry spells until it is established water it to ensure that the roots do not dry out. If two clematis are planted so that they should eventually dance together, keep the roots about 1m apart and incline their supporting canes towards each other.

Clematis appreciate showing their heads to the sun, while their roots prefer to be cool, as they are in the wild. Many patio gardeners find that they have ideal conditions when they plant a clematis in a gap along the paving, where the roots relish the cool dampness under stone while the shoots stretch to the sun. On open ground a brick or tile placed over the roots helps, but too often becomes a haven for snails.

Pruning

Pruning clematis is often presented as an arcane ritual whose correct observance is capable of being followed only by the few. In fact, it is incredibly simple. It all depends on when the clematis flowers. If the clematis flowers before midsummer, cut it back after flowering. If it flowers after midsummer, cut it back in the autumn or the following spring. Spring is usually recommended as being the better of these options, but if a clematis covered by dead leaves is shading a window then autumn pruning is preferable for aesthetic reasons. Varieties of *C. alpina* and *C. macropetala* are so modest in growth that they need no pruning at all.

The reason for pruning is simple: a clematis such as *C. armandii* is so vigorous that it leaps beyond its allotted span, climbs trees and weaves into any neighbour. This may be welcomed, in which case little is needed except cutting out the odd withered shoot. If unwelcome, the clematis should be pruned back after flowering, in the case of *C. armandii* and *C. montana*, to about 1m. One or two longer shoots may be left for training in specific places. This is a job for early summer. If performed in early spring, the flowering buds will be excised. When a vigorous clematis has been left unpruned for some years and has got completely out of hand, it is best not to cut it back in a single operation – it may die of shock.

Cut it back by a third one year and another third the next, to accustom it more gently.

A clematis like the large-flowered 'Marie Boisselot', flowering in both the first and the second half of the year, does not need massive pruning, merely some trimming and tidying up in spring. Vigorous clematis flowering in the second half of the year, 'Perle d'Azur', 'Comtesse de Bouchaud', *C. tangutica*, *C. orientalis*, *C. viticella* cultivars, *C. rehederiana* and the like, should be hard pruned to about 20cm from the ground in autumn or spring. If they are not, in the following year new growth will spring from the top of a jumbled bird's nest of tired old shoots and leaves. If they have been neglected for some years, again, it is safer not to cut them back entirely, but only by about a third at a time.

On the day the clematis are pruned they can be fed. Easiest is a handful of concentrated poultry manure such as 6X, lightly scratched into the soil.

CLIMBERS FOR THE SOUTH, EAST AND WEST

Wisteria sinensis, seen growing up stone houses built in the alkaline vineyards of France, is the most majestic of climbers, with its scented flowers falling in cascades in May, pinnate leaves through the summer, and even in winter a satisfying, sturdy outline. It likes sun and plenty of it. It is the ideal climber for an arbour or pergola, because the racemes fall down like chandeliers, and, unlike roses, do not attempt to stretch to the sun and become invisible below. After planting it is slow to flower, sometimes taking as long as five, even seven or eight years – longer if grown from seed. If after eight years it is still not flowering, this is nearly always because the bud wood is not getting sufficient sun. It should be moved to a sunnier spot. Should the tumescent buds get blasted by late frosts it will flower later but will lack the ethereal, lacy appearance of an earlier flowering without leaves. Up a south-facing wall it receives more protection than among railings or over an arbour assaulted on all sides by icy air. If frosted falling buds are a regular problem, it is best to replace it with the Japanese wisteria, *W. floribunda*, which comes into bud somewhat later and has slightly longer racemes but less scent. If in doubt

The trained frame of a white wisteria, Wisteria sinensis
'Alba'.

Wisteria sinensis *'Alba'.*

whether a plant is a Chinese or a Japanese wisteria,
see which way the shoots twine. Viewed from above,
Chinese wisteria twines clockwise and Japanese wisteria anticlockwise.

All wisterias are lovely, and white wisteria, either
W. sinensis 'Alba' or *W. floribunda* 'Alba', is the
loveliest of all. There are hybrid wisterias of various
colours, like *W.* × *formosa* 'Black Dragon' with purple pea flowers, and *W. s.* 'Pink Ice'. *W. floribunda*
'Multijuga' has long racemes so fat they almost
seem obscene. Wisteria needs a rich planting with
a handful of bonemeal or blood, fish and bone as
well as compost incorporated in the soil, and watering in dry weather until it is established. In its early
days, if the leaves seem yellowish and chloritic, a
dose of an iron-containing compound such as
Sequestrene will help, but, long-term, this expensive crutch should not be necessary.

Wisteria on a wall needs to be shaped into a firm
framework, with one of its shoots selected as a
leader, another kept as insurance and the others cut
back to four buds. In the following years further
shoots can be trained sideways along wires. If left
to its own devices wisteria becomes a mass of
whips. Once established, it needs both summer and
winter pruning, with new, unwanted shoots cut
back to about four buds. Although the tendrils
scroll round anything available, the main shoot
becomes in time a woody tree trunk; this means
that it can be grown as a standard, self-supporting
in time and looking incredibly pretty in the oriental mode both in and out of flower. The old wood
of wisteria has a remarkable capacity for regeneration, and, if long neglected and growing in all the
wrong directions, it nearly always sprouts again
after the most drastic carpentry. Then new shoots
can be trained where they are desired.

Like wisteria, laburnum with its falling racemes of
gold is invaluable for adorning tunnels, arbours and
pergolas where the flowers are viewed from below,

Lonicera etrusca *'Superba'*.

and the variety to get is *Laburnum × watereri* 'Vossii'. Its training is similar to that of wisteria.

There are legions of honeysuckles which enjoy sun and tolerate dry, alkaline conditions. They must have good planting and the more compost incorporated, the better they will flower. The early Dutch honeysuckle, *Lonicera periclymenum* 'Belgica', is an improved version of our wild plant, with larger flowers, blooming in May and June. *L. p.* 'Serotina' flowers later and is equally good, as is *L. p.* 'Heaven Scent' which has creamy white flowers throughout the summer and into autumn. *L. etrusca* is utterly lovely with perfoliate leaves like collars round the stem from which emerge the heads of fragrant, cream flowers. It is vigorous, and it is important to cater for its ultimate height which may reach 4m.

The delight of summer jasmine, *Jasminum officinalis*, comes on a June night when its scent permeates the darkness, luring moths for pollination. The basic white type is far better than the pinkish *J. stephanense*. Once established, it can be cut back in spring or on a mild winter's day to the height required. It can take east- and west-facing aspects, but is happiest in full sun. It has no objection to alkalinity, but will appreciate annual feeding, and the deeper and moister the soil the better it will flower. *Trachelospermum asiaticum* is slightly similar to jasmine, its flowers have a yellow hue and its smell is intense but it is much more tender.

A fine climber for a sunny spot is *Solanum crispum* 'Glasnevin', with mounds of yellow-centred, mauve potato flowers for weeks and even months in June and July. It can be tied to a trellis, and, to prevent undue woodiness, about a third of the oldest growth cut to the ground in spring. Its white counterpart, *S. laxum* 'Album', is just as prolific, though rather more tender. The only drawback of these solanums is that one goes to sniff, thinking that, surely such lovely blooms, particularly the white, should be scented, but never a whiff at all.

It is small wonder that the Russian vine, *Polygonum baldschuanicum*, is called 'Mile a Minute'. It is the favourite of beginners who thrill at a climber displaying drapes of white flowers so easily. It grows in any soil, takes any aspect and survives the coldest winter. What more could one want? A lot. Soon everyone tires of its clumsy invasion of space and switches to something better behaved.

Akebia quinata is scented and exquisite, but not for those who like their plants flashy. It has dainty, lobed leaves and in early summer bears first female flowers, maroon with fat sticky styles, followed by male, pale pink with dark stamens. It threads its way up wires on a wall and requires little in the way of maintenance other than its being cut back when it gets out of hand.

Not widely grown, but with an intensely strong scent of chocolate, is the evergreen *Stauntonia hexaphylla*, which in early summer bears small flowers,

Akebia quinata.

pale pink outside and deep red inside. It is named after Sir Leonard Staunton, who, with his little son George acting as page, went with Lord MacCartney on an unsuccessful trading mission to China in the eighteenth century and collected plants all the way. It does not object to being cut back and in winter provides a welcome green. In a frost pocket, a late frost may cull the flower buds.

The blue passion flower, *Passiflora caerula*, does well in alkaline soils, but succumbs to a tough winter. Grown in the soil of a cold greenhouse, it produces a series of its incredible flowers – used by the Jesuits in South America to teach Christ's passion on the cross, the three stigmas being the three nails, the five anthers the five wounds, the corona Christ's halo and the ten petals the apostles, Peter and Judas being absent – and, through runners, tries to colonize the ground outside. Sometimes it produces a pure white sport, which is sold under the name of 'Constance Elliot'. A nice purple variety growing as eagerly is *P. racemosa*.

The pleasure of *Actinidia kolomikta* comes from its leaves, which, on a mature plant, are white, pink and green. Although the variegation fades towards the end of the season, it remains longer than the colour of most flowers. The only trouble about this climber is that its eagerness to come into leaf may cause, in a frost pocket, the unfurling foliage to get blasted not once but twice, in which case the plant does not necessarily die but creeps on from year to year, weakened. It needs a sheltered spot, not necessarily sunny, but protected from late frosts.

If there is a shed to be covered, *Celastrus orbiculatus* is worth considering. It twines its way up the nearest support, growing rapidly. The flowers are negligible but the leaves in autumn are gold, and among them are bright yellow fruit capsules which open to reveal scarlet seeds. It is best in a place where it can ramble unpruned.

CLIMBERS FOR SHADE

Several climbers such as ivy and *Hydrangea anomala* subsp. *petiolaris* attach themselves to the wall by sticky pads on aerial roots. This should do a building no harm as long as the mortar is tight and the bricks not crumbling. In the driest, darkest and most alkaline conditions ivy can perform an all-year cosmetic job on an ugly building. It is one of the few plants which can grow in the shade of a yew, as long as a green variety like the pointed *Hedera helix* 'Sagittifolia' is planted. There are good variegated ivies, for instance *H. h.* 'Goldheart' and *H. h.* 'Sagittifolla Variegata' with silver edging, but they need a modicum of light to keep their two colours. *H. h.* 'Buttercup' makes it seem as if the sun were shining on a dark winter's day, but it has slightly contradictory

Golden ivy, Hedera helix *'Buttercup', in January; to the left is a cob house with flint and brick base.*

requirements, needing sun to develop its golden leaves, but too much – as with many gold plants – can scorch its delicate skin. Growing against an open west or east wall gives it enough light to keep its colour. Although wild ivy is a fast grower, patience is needed with the gold and variegated varieties which may take more than a couple of years to get established, in due course quietly clinging to the wall. With the variegated ivies, watch for reversions to plain green and cut them out. If in time the ivy bushes out too far, trim it with a hedge trimmer in spring.

Virginia creeper, *Parthenocissus quinquefolia*, is an old standby for covering houses and large buildings, green in summer, fire in autumn and bristly brown stems through the winter. It is not fussy about soil or aspect and can take a north wall, although if asked it prefers the sun. It takes about two years to get going and then often outgrows its allotted space. When pruning, allow a margin of at least 0.5m from the roof, window and gutters. Very pretty and completely hardy is Chinese Virginia creeper, *P. henryana*, with beautiful leaves showing silver veins, and in autumn turning purple then scarlet. It has no objection to alkalinity, but does like a moister soil.

Hydrangea anomala subsp. *petiolaris* is a brilliant plant for a shady wall. It has large, white flower bracts in June and bright green foliage which birds love to nest in. Other hydrangeas may prefer a more acid soil, but this climber is completely at home in lime. Over the years it will need to be clipped from gutters and windows. *Schizophragma hydrangeoides* is a fancier and fussier version of *Hydrangea anomala* subsp. *petiolaris*, with large, heart-shaped, cream bracts in midsummer, and it really likes a touch more light to do well.

Hydrangea anomala *subsp.* petiolaris, *with rose 'Paul Transom'.*

Schizophragma hydrangeoides.

WALL SHRUBS

The soil beside walls is usually dryer than that nearby and the aspect more sheltered. Many shrubs and trees appreciate its protection, a fact that kitchen gardeners have realized for centuries. Espalier pears and cordon apples, fan-trained cherries, plums and peaches, are all trees which naturally grow as standards but are superb as wall shrubs and available trained from garden centres and the catalogues of fruit growers such as Ken Muir. Basking in the wall's warmth, they are less likely to be blasted by late frosts and will fruit earlier. On the right rootstock, they are tailored for the space available. If peaches succumb to leaf curl they may be sprayed or sheltered from leaf-curl spores with sheets of plastic in early spring; but in this case they are not really worth the effort of growing.

Outside kitchen concerns, a shrub such as rosemary can be pinned and trained on a wall, and so can *Deutzia* and numerous others. It is a matter of experimenting – tying back taller shoots at the back and excising shoots jutting forward. Soon the plant gets the message and does what it is told. *Ceanothus*, particularly the more tender and early flowering evergreen varieties, can be grown informally against a wall, where it forms blue clouds in late spring, or tied to a frame of wires or wood, where it is clipped and tied back after flowering to give a wallpaper effect.

Moroccan broom, *Cytisus battandieri*, may be grown in sheltered places as a freestanding shrub, but it is more than happy leaning against a south- or west-facing wall, where in June, about four years after planting, its racemes of yellow flowers give out a powerful fragrance of pineapple. Its felted, grey-green leaves are lovely all year. Like *Ceanothus*, it can be grown informally with occasional support, or tied to wires and clipped tight after flowering.

Abutilon × suntense 'Jermyns', one of the hardiest of these tender shrubs, survives outside against a south- or west-facing wall and produces a succession of pale amethyst saucer flowers. Occasional stems can be tied to the wall. It is not long lived, odd stems dying each year and the whole plant rarely lasting more than seven or eight years, but it is fast growing and magnificent for weeks in summer. When happy, it may self-seed.

Carpenteria californica, with its white petals and frizzy, yellow stamens is another slightly tender shrub which can survive in a sunny sheltered spot. It looks best when tied fan-shaped to wires on a wall. *Chaenomeles speciosa* 'Moorloosei', a Japanese quince with pink and white waxy blossom, is also best trained fan-shaped against a wall, but it is totally hardy and takes any aspect, sun or shade, with equanimity.

The evergreen *Magnolia grandiflora* looks so exotic, not just the large, glossy leaves but the huge

Seedlings of Abutilon × suntense *'Jermyns', and a white abutilon in Northamptonshire.*

Forsythia suspense, with yew and holly buttresses at Hinton Ampner gardens, Hampshire.

BELOW: Garrya elliptica *on north-facing wall in February.*

creamy bowls in August with their dangerously seductive smell, that one would guess it to be an acid lover with very precise requirements. In fact, it is tolerant of most soils and, given plenty of compost and manure at the time of planting, will thrive against a south- or west-facing wall. It requires no pruning.

Another sun-loving shrub is *Fremontodendron* 'California Glory'. It is hardy, taking severe winters in its stride but objecting to a frost pocket where late blasts after warm spells will shrivel emerging buds and leaves. A succession of them may kill the plant. It takes extreme alkalinity and, when settled, it produces a succession of shiny, gold flowers for weeks on end. The only thing to watch for is dust from the stems, which can cause skin irritation.

Cape figwort, *Phygelius capensis*, is a curious little number, late flowering with long lobes like a fuchsia, which may be dusty red with a gold interior, plain yellow or green. It is more than happy against a sunny wall, enjoying limy soils so much that its creeping roots may spread too far. But if it invades, the shallow roots are easily pulled out.

Some wall shrubs are so willing to grow that they are taken for granted, but stalwarts such as *Cotoneaster horizontalis* should never be despised. This neat plant requires no tying or training and rests its curved, gleaming stems against a wall of any aspect, producing tiny flowers visited by bees in summer and red berries taken by birds in winter. It needs no pruning other than to cut off odd shoots

which leap from the wall. As easily and widely grown and accepting all aspects, is *Jasminum nudiflorum* with starry yellow flowers in December – and what amazement it must have caused when it was introduced from China by Robert Fortune in Victorian times. All this needs is to be cut back in March to a tighter fit against the wall. Even a neglected *J. nudiflorum* reaching 1m from the wall can be cut back to 20cm without harm.

Few regard forsythia as a garden essential, yet *Forsythia suspensa* with its long, lax shoots is ideal for growing up a north-facing wall and round a door-way. It can face south too, and in the National Trust garden at Hinton Ampner, Hampshire, a long wall intermittently buttressed by pillars of holly and yew turns gold with its flowers.

Another shrub for a north-facing wall is the ever-green *Garrya elliptica* and here the best variety is 'James Roof', producing long catkins in January, as exquisite as the carved tassels on Hepplewhite chairs. Sometimes in a severe winter its leaves get scorched and the catkins are halted in mid growth. When this occurs, these can be cut back in April to the fresh-ly emerging growth.

Firethorn, *Pyracantha*, is popular with flowers similar to hawthorn attracting bees, followed by a mass of berries which may be red, yellow or orange. The names 'Golden Charmer', 'Golden Sun', 'Orange Charmer', 'Orange Glow' and 'Soleil d'Or' say it all. It can take any aspect, but without sun it will produce fewer berries. It needs to tied back for a tight display. It can also be grown as a hedge. Its only disadvantage is its thorniness which means that it should not be grown close to any door. Pruning is best in late winter at the end of the berry display and before the flower buds are forming.

Not widely grown, but one of the most attractive and amenable of wall shrubs for dry, alkaline soils is *Ribes speciosum*. Sometimes its red hanging flow-ers, displayed from late February to May or even

Ribes speciosum: *this hardy wall shrub can take any aspect and bears fuchsia-like flowers from late February to May.*

June, are mistaken for fuchsia, but its rounded leaves, tiny balls of glossy fruit and prickles confirm its membership of the gooseberry family. It takes any aspect, and all it needs is to be tied back to wires. When the side shoots are trained horizontal-ly the dangling flowers show their best.

PLANTING

Pruning may be forgotten, watering may be unpunc-tual, but what a plant will not forgive is mean plant-ing. Dig a hole at least four times, more on light soil, larger than the pot containing the roots and incorpo-rate compost, home-made or bought, manure if avail-able, a handful of blood, fish and bone, if around, or a handful of bonemeal to help the plant's structure, and incorporate this into the soil. When planting against an aspect which gets little rain, usually east, or near another shrub, leave a 1m gap from the wall or shrub so that the young roots will have sufficient space to stretch. Leave a saucer-shaped depression around the plant for ease of watering during dry periods

PERENNIALS

Most perennials die back in September, giving us a chance to see the view, imagine improvements to them, and keep them under control when they emerge in spring.

Mounds of everlasting sweet pea, *Lathyrus lati-folius*, lacking scent, give a regular display with con-siderably less cosseting than the annual, fragrant sweet pea, and the colours, pink, pink and violet, mauve and white are lovely. It can be raised from seed or propagated by division in autumn or spring. The golden hop, *Humulus lupulus*, is bright and reli-able and can clothe an arbour, in autumn covering it with papery fruit which can be used for making beer. It sprawls around and is not for those who like their gardens tidy. It is propagated by division. Climbing monkshood, raised from seed, will give hooded flowers in autumn. Variegated periwinkle, *Vinca major* 'Variegata', usually grown as ground cover, is a surprisingly pretty low climber with ever-green leaves and large, blue flowers as early as Jan-uary. When it is too happy it can become invasive.

CHAPTER 5

Roses

Virtually all the classic roses of the twentieth century, the hybrid teas and the scentless floribundas, demand a rich, clay soil and frequent sprayings to flower well and continuously. The new millennium has a different agenda. Today's gardeners want scented roses which stay disease-free without a heavy regime of sprays. Breeders have responded, and most newly introduced roses have not only scent but a sound constitution which can take all soils including alkaline ones. Many species and historic roses have been grown on these soils for centuries. When selecting roses from catalogues, the words to note are: vigorous, sturdy, tough, disease-free, and strong and healthy. In poorer soils roses are about 20 per cent smaller in size, and the species and once-flowering shrub roses may be more successful than repeat flowering varieties.

When it comes to colour, on a chalk or lime soil some reds may be bleached and the tones less saturated than on more neutral or acid soils. The rich, veined salmon 'Pink Meidiland' becomes a delicate peach-pink with white veins.

The roses available today are sold budded to the roots of *Rosa laxa* or *R. rubinigosa*. This is done for convenience and speed of propagation, although many roses, including the species, most ramblers and climbers, the gallicas and rugosas, given the chance, grow well on their own roots, and indeed, these may take over from the bud wood. This means that cuttings will grow satisfactorily; just after flowering is a good time to take them, with the plant in reproductive mode. Other intensively bred roses lack the innate vigour to survive or to give a decent showing on their own roots and need to stand on the feet of the more robust *R. rubinigosa*.

OPPOSITE PAGE: Rosa moyesii *'Geranium', in flower.*

RAMBLER ROSES

Today's ramblers have been developed from species such as *R. multiflora*, the glossy-leaved *R. wichurana* and *R. banksiae*, introduced from western China in the nineteenth century. In the wild they scramble through trees and shrubs, but although their flexible shoots bend naturally, up buildings they are best pinned into position while they are still growing – older stems may split and snap.

Ramblers in the garden can bend over arches, clothe sheds and garages and swing from trees giving a sense of total embowerment. The fact that they are nearly all only summer flowering should never be regretted – their charm comes, not just from the mass of small flowers held in large bunches, but the long leaves, the graceful growth pattern, the hips and the relentless dynamic of their continuous change. They do well on alkaline soils, and the hips of the single ramblers – those with only five petals – often throw seedlings.

Some of the giant ramblers, growing up to 10m, are: the superb 'Wedding Day', rich cream fading to white and then blushing to pink, with single petals and later many hips; 'Rambling Rector', semi-double white; 'Ethel', known more grandly in France as 'Princess Louise', pink which looks well against purple foliage; 'Bobbie James', white; and the biggest of all, 'Kiftsgate'. Avoid growing these where they will feel confined; like a small archway up which the rose will want to outstretch, or up a small fruit tree which may be hugged to death. At Kiftsgate in Gloucestershire 'Kiftsgate' flowers from the heights of a beech tree. Sturdy buildings are suitable, as are hedges of the Leyland cypress. If the rambler is to grow up a tree, plant it where the prevailing wind, usually west, will blow it against the tree, and in a hole about 1m from the

Rose 'Ethel' growing up purple-leaved Prunus.

Rose 'Kiftsgate' on apple tree; later the tree fell and the rose had to be cut down.

tree trunk – this will ensure that it gets slightly more moisture. The rambler may take up to five years to make headway, but then will claw its path to the sky.

Ramblers of all sizes may be trained spreadeagled against walls, where fanned or horizontally-trained shoots will produce more blooms than if they are allowed to follow their inclination and grow straight up. Roses growing considerably tall but not reaching marathon heights are: the moonlight mauve 'Sir Cedric Morris'; 'Albéric Barbier', creamy white and sometimes with a second crop; the perennially popular 'Albertine', with salmon-red buds; and the similar but superior 'François Juranville', with quilled petals.

Smaller ramblers like the lovely 'Phyllis Bide', with pink buds turning to rosy gold flowers, can be grown over arches and will not reach too high. At Mottisfont Abbey in Hampshire the rambler 'Sanders White' is grown pinned down with mauve footballs of *Allium christophii* growing through it.

The scent of the species ramblers usually comes from the central style rather than the petals and this means that many of their double-flowered progeny, such as 'Dorothy Perkins', without a style lack fragrance. For fragrance, it is best to sniff out the ramblers first in a garden such as Mottisfont Abbey or Queen Mary's Rose Garden in Regent's Park in London.

CLIMBERS AND PILLAR ROSES

Climbing roses are usually sports – mutations – from bush roses which have decided to grow and grow. Because of their vigour, they nearly always do well on poorer soils, making the most of what they have. The flowers are usually large and the stems stout and stiff, not amenable to rigorous training but happy up walls.

Taller climbers, all suitable for growing up houses, are: the gorgeous 'Climbing Étoile d'Hollande', deep red and scented; 'Guinée', very similar; and 'Climbing Mme Caroline Testout', rose-pink. The flowers of the apricot 'Climbing Lady Hillingdon' droop and look down at people below, a positive advantage in a climber. This rose needs a warm, sheltered wall.

If roses are grown up a wall of limited height, choose pillar roses, ones that will not have to be continually cut back. Good pillar roses are: 'Maigold', bronze-yellow with golden stamens; 'Climbing Iceberg', bravely repeating for months (some gardeners even complain of its factory production); 'Aloha', with old-fashioned pink flowers; and sturdy 'Parkdirektor Riggers', deep crimson. 'Zephirine Drouin',

an old Bourbon hybrid from the nineteenth century, is the original 'Rose without a Thorn' and, although its pink is slightly garish and its leaves have a tendency to mildew, it is a reliable and continuously scented bloomer and grown near a door, will not snag at the clothing of passers-by. Flesh pink 'New Dawn' is more supple than most climbers and will bend over arches, and, like the more recently introduced pinky champagne 'Penny Lane', continues through the summer. Two roses, once-flowering and worth growing are 'Constance Spry', rounded cabbage blooms with a musk smell, and 'Alchymist', whose golden flowers flecked with orange change tones from day to day. 'Pink Perpétue' is a well-mannered, medium-sized climber producing a succession of neat, clear pink flowers, which, after their performance, tidily drop their petals.

As a shrub, 'Little White Pet' is small with pink buds and white flowers; but in its incarnation as 'Félicite et Perpétué' it will cover a sizeable wall.

Rose 'Maigold'.

Likewise as a shrub 'Cécile Brunner', with tiny buds fit for a doll's house, is often reluctant to perform, but as 'Climbing Cécile Brunner' it becomes vigorous and an ideal cover for walls and arches since its stems are as pliable as any rambler's. Both can take a north-facing wall, as can the coppery pink 'Paul Transom' and the old, creamy 'Mme Alfred Carrière'. Take care that their tips do not top the walls, because if they catch a glimpse of the sun they will flower only there. They can be cut back, but 'Mme Alfred Carrière' does not take happily to overmuch pruning.

HISTORIC ROSES

The oldest garden rose in cultivation, grown by the Romans and the Greeks, and probably the Medes and Persians before them, is the scented *Rosa gallica officinalis*, known since medieval times as the 'Apothecary's Rose' – its petals were infused in water to cure numerous complaints. It flowers for about three weeks around midsummer, like most old roses, and is semi-double with deep cerise blooms. It bears a wealth of symbolism: it was the red rose of Lancaster and is the flower of the Virgin Mary and many saints, and before them was the flower of Venus, goddess of love. 'Rosamunda', a mutation of the 'Apothecary's Rose' to which it may occasionally revert, has striped petals and is another ancient rose, while 'Robert le Diable', flowering slightly later, is not startling at a distance, but close up its exquisite flecks of pink, red, mauve, purple and white can be appreciated. All the gallicas are at their best at midsummer. Although sold budded to alien rootstock, they are more than happy growing on their own roots, where they sucker, but not invasively.

Another group of old roses are the albas, all white or palest pink and only once flowering. These include: the pink rose known since medieval times as 'Maiden's Blush' (in France 'Cuisse de Nymph'

Roses, including 'Rose de Rescht' in an Oxfordshire garden designed by Sir Hardy Amies in 1973.

– 'Maiden's Thigh'); the 'White Rose of York', also the white rose of the Jacobites; creamy 'Mme Plantier'; 'Königin van Dänemark' or 'Queen of Denmark', pink with a neat central button; and perhaps the loveliest of the group, the informal blush pink 'Céleste' also known as 'Celestial'. The albas usually grow taller than the gallicas, can even flower in dappled shade and their leaves have a blue tinge when compared with the pea-green leaves of the gallicas. If they seem gawky at the base, smaller roses, or grey-leaved plants such as lavender, rosemary or senecio can be grown in front of them.

The damask roses, said to have been introduced from Damascus by the crusaders, are the most scented of the old roses, but only in ideal conditions. They can be temperamental and need a hot summer to do well.

For repeat flowering old roses, it is worth growing the Portlands introduced in the early nineteenth century. 'Comte de Chambord' has generous pink buds, and 'Jacques Cartier' a mass of imbricated (overlapping like tiles) pink petals like a whirlpool. The best old rose always in flower is 'Rose de Rescht', reddish purple with healthy leaves.

The hybrid perpetuals, developed in Victorian times, are not perpetual in the modern sense but remontant, with two or three flowerings; they need to be cut back, to about the fourth leaf, when dead heading to encourage further buds. Excellent varieties are 'Mme Pierre Oger', white getting pinker with age, the slate-grey 'Reine des Violettes', and 'Ferdinand Pichard,' like a stripy 'Rosamunda'.

The early twentieth-century Pemberton hybrid musks are scented roses with an attractive, informal habit which mix well with other shrubs. They usually carry on flowering through the summer. 'Buff Beauty', a rich yellow biscuit, can grow up a wall. Other good hybrid musks are 'Penelope', shell pink fading to white, salmon pink 'Cornelia' and 'Felicia', rose pink with a touch of apricot.

RUGOSA ROSES

Magenta *R. rugosa*, from the sandy shores of Japan and the colder parts of north-east China, flowers continually through the summer and is particularly good in cold areas. Although said not to, it tolerates poor soils, including the alkaline, with equanimity. It seems to appreciate their typical lightness. Its petals are delicately crumpled like tissue paper and its robust, leathery leaves laugh at blackspot and mildew. In autumn it produces a mass of tomato-sized hips among buds which are still flowering. The orange hips and purple petals of 'Scabrosa' make a garish partnership, while the hips and white petals of *R. rugosa* 'Alba' make a pleasing but less startling contrast.

This informal rose and its progeny are accommodating and happy in a mixed shrub border or at the back of a border of perennials. Good reliable varieties are: 'Fru Dagmar Hastrup', with large, single, pale pink petals like shells; 'Roseraie de l'Häye', purple; and 'Blanche Double de Coubert', white. Pink 'Martin Frobisher' from Canada is excellent, as is 'Mrs Doreen Pike'. Good performers, although scentless, are 'Pink Grootendorst', with pinked edges, and the similar but blush pink 'Fimbriata'. 'Sarah van Fleet' tends to be disappointing on alkaline soils.

The single varieties produce the most hips, and, when this fails to occur, it is nearly always due to lack of moisture. If some hips are collected in autumn and left outside during winter, the following spring the seed can be sown. From germination it takes about three years to flower and tends to come true from the parent, seedlings from 'Blanche Double de Coubert' flowering semi-double white and those from the species *R. rugosa* flowering single magenta.

HYBRID TEA ROSES AND FLORIBUNDA ROSES

Hybrid tea roses, now officially named Bush roses, do not perform outstandingly in dry, highly alkaline soils, and in cases where they do flourish they have always been given a virtual change of soil. Some of the more forgiving, including several scented varieties, do their best; it is a matter of trial and error. Regular spraying is recommended. Modern introductions tend to be healthier and stronger than the earlier ones. Hybrid teas do not blend well with other plants in a mixed border and are best grown in a formal rose garden or the kitchen garden for cutting.

David Austin rose, 'Mayflower'.

David Austin rose 'English Garden'.

The floribundas, less scented, make their effect in massed planting. White 'Iceberg', yellow 'Chinatown' and red 'Frensham' are all vigorous and require less spraying and care than the average hybrid tea.

MODERN SHRUB ROSES

Most modern shrub roses have a sound constitution, giving a good performance through the season. They may be grown with other shrubs, but they do need sufficient room to display their blooms unhampered. Larger, once-flowering roses, probably best on their own because of their reach, are: 'Cerise Bouquet', scentless but with attractive arching shoots and each flower backed by a rounded bract; 'Nevada', with huge, single cream petals 9cm across; and 'Golden Wings', yellow petals contrasting with mahogany stamens. Other shrub roses are continually in bloom, like the lemon yellow 'Leverkusen', and 'Fred Loads', bright orange looking splendid at a distance, particularly against a dark background of laurel. Many a scarlet-flowered shrub considered garish close to looks striking at the end of the garden.

Good and healthy, medium-sized shrub roses are 'Smarty', with dainty, continuous 'wild rose' flowers, and 'Rose Gaujard', rich pink petals with a silver reverse, with little scent but one of the few roses of classic hybrid tea form to flourish on highly alkaline soils without intensive care. Perhaps the most outstanding performer is the pink 'Bonica', which cheerfully produces its blooms throughout the season. 'Bonica' is effective as a standard at the back of a flower border where it lends height to a mass of herbaceous plants.

For the smaller garden, some healthy little roses have been introduced in recent years. They include: 'Flower Carpet', cerise and repeat flowering with glossy, green leaves; 'Flower Carpet White', identical except for the flowers; and 'Marjorie Fair', with single, white-edged, carmine petals. A yellow version of 'Flower Carpet' is also available. There are good roses as well which have been around for some time, like 'Ballerina', with continuous, hydrangea-like heads of single pink flowers with white centres, followed by hips; rich lilac 'Yesterday'; and 'The Fairy', with sprays of pink pompons.

DAVID AUSTIN'S ENGLISH ROSES

David Austin's early roses needed a rich diet and a heavy soil to survive, let alone flourish, and few were happy on alkaline soils, particularly chalk ones, but some of his latest introductions have excellent constitutions and will grow anywhere. His roses are scented, each with a unique fragrance. Their beauty, as with most roses, comes from the individual flower rather than the shape and habit of the bush itself. Some of the best Austin roses are: blush 'Heritage', with cabbage-shaped blooms and the myrrh-scented, golden 'English Garden'; peachy 'Sharifa Asma'; pink and single 'Lucetta', taller than the others; and the rich biscuit yellow 'Sweet Juliet'. They are all continuous flowering, as is the sturdy pink 'Mayflower', which makes a good showing even on poor soil. So does 'Shropshire Lass', once flowering.

ROSA PIMPINELLIFOLIA (*ROSA SPINOSISSIMA*) – SCOTTISH OR BURNET ROSES

These sturdy, prickly and beautiful little roses with ferny leaves and dense growth are hybrids from a wild rose growing from Britain to the Caucasus. They are summer flowering and thrive in the poorest conditions. They are often sold on their own roots, but this may permit them to sucker invasively and they are kept under better control when rooted to alien rootstock. Attractive varieties are the yellow 'Dunwich Rose', discovered at Dunwich in Suffolk, and 'Mary, Queen of Scots', purple and grey. Sometimes they send up seedlings, each with a unique shape and charm.

One exception to the rule of summer flowering is 'Stanwell's Perpetual', growing to about 1m and studded with informal, pink flowers all summer long. It has a slight inclination to rust. Another exception is a recent introduction, 'Lochinvar', blush pink and double. These need more feeding than the once-flowering varieties.

SPECIES ROSES

There are nearly 300 species roses growing wild in the northern hemisphere, and most are too large to be grown with rose cultivars, and are either too casual or lacking sufficient character for the garden. Some fine exceptions have a grace of habit which makes them welcome even when flowerless.

R. xanthina f. *hugonis* is usually the first rose to open in May, with curving stems and little, primrose cups appearing on tufts of bright, ferny foliage. *R. xanthina* 'Canary Bird', with bright yellow flowers is one of its offspring. 'Geranium', a cultivar of *R. moyesii*, is a tall species, stiffly upright, with ferny leaves and large, single flowers of a soft yet bright metallic red, contrasting with gold stamens. Later its hips are large, glistening and with a shapely waist. If hips fail to appear, it is nearly always after a dry summer and due to lack of moisture, as noted above.

R. glauca, found growing wild in the Pyrenees, has grey leaves on arching plum stems and little, pink flowers followed by a mass of red hips which often germinate below. It makes a gentle foil to other shrubs and roses, and flower arrangers love it. A larger species, *R. fedtschenkoana*, at least 3m

Rosa moyesii *'Geranium', with hips.*

high, has similar glaucous leaves and small, single, white flowers which appear intermittently through the season. Sometimes its own roots take over, suckering considerably.

Rosa × odorata 'Mutabilis', also known as 'Changeable Chinaman' and the 'Butterfly Rose', has a curious charm with its twisted petals which are deep yellow in bud, open gold pink and then turn to a deeper pink and finally cerise before they fall. The petals of the European gallicas, with their reddish tones, fade with age, but those of the China roses deepen from pale to dark tones. *R. × o.* 'Mutabilis' rarely has hips in northern climates and needs a warm sheltered site to flourish, but, unlike most species, continues flowering for weeks, even months.

Although the leaves of the sweetbriar, *R. rubiginosa*, produce a welcome scent in rain and damp, it is really too ungainly for gardens, and the Penzance sweetbriar hybrids rarely flourish in alkaline soils. However, one worthy performer is the old sweetbriar 'Mannings Blush', with small, pink, double flowers. 'Duplex', usually known as 'Wolley Dod's Rose', is a large, nicely shaped shrub with semi-double, soft pink flowers and green-grey leaves which exude a slight fragrance when rubbed. Later it bears large, rather prickly hips. Another rose with scented leaves in damp weather is the 'Incense Rose', *R. primula*, a medium-sized shrub with soft yellow flowers. The leaves after rain or when rubbed smell like St Peter's at Rome on a particularly holy day.

One rose not grown for flowers or leaves but for its viciously spiked stems is *R. sericea* subsp. *omeiensis* var. *pteracantha*. It has pleasant, single, white flowers

Rose 'Duplex', usually known as 'Wolley Dodd's Rose'; this is a good-sized, shrub rose, here grown urn-shaped between five splayed posts.

and the bright ferny foliage of so many species, and then the new red shoots develop thorns like the silhouettes of waves, translucent coral against the light.

PLANTING

Select a site with at least a few hours of sun each day where the roots of the rose will not be in competition with other plants; the ramblers to grow up trees are an exception. All roses should be planted in a hole with the budded union between roots and shoots, a lumpy swelling, about 6cm below the soil level. Incorporate plenty of compost, rotted manure if available, a handful of poultry manure pellets if not, and a handful of bonemeal in the soil, and spread out the roots.

Whether roses arrive container-grown or bare-rooted in winter seems to make little difference to subsequent growth. If they arrive bare-rooted when it is inconvenient to plant them, dig a hole and heel them in the ground. It is essential that the roots should never dry out.

If you are planting roses in ground where they have previously been grown, replace the soil or, quicker, sterilize it with diluted disinfectant to clear any residual fungi. A well-known household disinfectant will do this, although it is no longer permitted to state the fact on its label.

DISEASE

To spray or not to spray? Nearly all the roses mentioned above have been grown satisfactorily on a chalk soil with a pH of 8.5 and without spraying. At the end of the season many show a slight but tolerable degree of blackspot. No one wants to nurse a ward of sickly patients, and if a rose is heavily infected with blackspot, mildew or rust, the best action is to burn it and invest in a healthier variety. At one stage, an ancient 'Dorothy Perkins' grown on its own roots was as white as a ghost with mildew, and the following winter dug out. A small piece of root was inadvertently left in the soil and the following year sent out a shoot. Within three years 'Dorothy Perkins' was flowering again, and since then has never shown any sign of mildew.

Obviously, the plant was rejuvenated by growing a new root system. Mildew is a fungal complaint often caused by lack of moisture, and is also the sign of a plant under pressure.

A survey in *Gardening Which* showed that to grow chives nearby alleviates blackspot. If spraying is considered necessary, Roseclear 3 is the best all-round spray for diseases and aphids. For rust alone use Systhane.

FEEDING

The species roses can survive without feeding, but all roses really appreciate a yearly feed, the richer the better. Give each a handful of 6X, DUG or another of the composts from concentrated chicken manure, plus a spadeful or more of any available manure or compost.

PRUNING

The best time for tidying up ramblers is autumn, when they are still in leaf but have finished growing. A rambler with several shoots can have two or three old, woody stems cut back to ground level to encourage new shoots, and be given a light trim. The new season's shoots can be tied in to stop them from getting battered by winter storms.

It is rarely practicable to prune giant ramblers roosting in trees. An occasional dead shoot can be yanked down by using a ladder and pole.

When it comes to summer-flowering shrub roses, they need little attention and can be given a light prune after they have flowered, or on a mild day from late winter to early spring, with two or three old stems cut out at the base. If they are producing hips, late winter is the time for this tidying up. The repeat-flowering bush and shrub roses can be cut down to about half their height at any time from late winter to early April, and any dead, weak or twiggy growth cut away.

R. sericea subsp. *omeiensis* var. *pteracantha* requires a pruning in late winter or spring, since only the stems of the current season's growth are coral coloured. Each stem should be reduced to about a third of its height.

CHAPTER 6

Bulbs, Corms and Rhizomes

Bulbs spring up like urns, opening strap or spade leaves to receive the rising buds. Most are more than happy on chalky and limestone soils, appreciating their good drainage and never, as they can on clay or water-logged soils, rotting in winter. One of the best places for early flowering bulbs is under a deciduous tree such as a beech, *Gingko*, *Cercis* or *Catalpa*. The bulbs give a carpet of colour streaked with the shadows of branches, and later fade as the tree comes into leaf.

It is best to buy most bulbs and tubers in their dormant stage – for daffodils and other spring bulbs in autumn, and later-flowering bulbs like crinum lilies in early spring. However, they are widely available container-grown when flowering, which means that you see exactly what you are getting, but at greater expense. Some bulbs, snowdrops, bluebells and winter aconites are best bought 'green' just after flowering. A number of nurserymen listed in *The Plantfinder* supply them.

Several bulbs and tubers widely considered tender will survive fairly cold winters when given protection, and one of the easiest methods is a gravel garden, with or without a plastic membrane. The mulch of gravel acts as a blanket in winter and in summer it prevents the plants from drying out. Another advantage is that darker plants, whose charm comes from delicate detail, show up better against pale gravel.

When choosing bulbs, the temptation is to try as many varieties as possible, but, for effect, it is better to have ten, or a hundred – a thousand, if there is room – of the same together rather than one or two each of twenty species.

OPPOSITE PAGE:
Narcissus *'Jenny' under an ancient, purple-leaved* Prunus.

NATURALIZING

When naturalizing bulbs, plant a minimum of fifty to give them a chance of establishing a self-sustaining colony. Throw them on the ground and plant them where they lie. This avoids a geometric pattern and gives a natural grouping fading towards the edges.

PLANTING

Plant the bulb with its top about twice its length deep in the soil. Exceptions such as the Madonna lily, *Lilium candidum*, and nerine lilies, which like to be planted in a shallow fashion, or the rhizomes of the bearded iris best anchored on the soil surface, are mentioned separately. The fact is, when happy, bulbs find their optimum level, shifting up or down according to their needs.

Cylindrical bulb planters with battlemented edges are widely available for planting in grass. The edges are pressed down, a gobbet of turf removed, the bulb laid down and the turf replaced. Another method is cutting and rolling back turf, putting the bulbs down, and then relaying the turf. However, these methods are not practicable for the lone gardener planting vast numbers of bulbs, and, just as effective, much easier and taking less time is getting a spade, slicing it into the turf and levering it to and fro, slipping about four bulbs along the open slice and then stamping the turf shut.

MAINTENANCE

Before the bulbs have finished flowering, a sprinkling of sulphate of potash on a windless day helps to ensure that none come up blind the following year.

When the flowers are over the question is whether to cut back or not cut back? Several authorities say it is best to dead head, so that the plant's energies are forced into fattening the bulbs rather than producing seed. In fact, dead heading is impracticable with large numbers of bulbs and seems to make little difference to their flowering the subsequent year, although near the house it may be required for aesthetic reasons. As for leaves, let them die of their own accord and leave uncut until about six weeks after the flowers have finished. This means that a lot of browning foliage is flopping on the border. To mask this, bulbs can be grown beside later perennials or have lavender or sage in front of them or if, like *Camassia* and daffodils, they are robust, to naturalize them in drifts in grass.

PLANT LIST

The list below is not exhaustive, and many bulbs and tubers are left unmentioned, like *Anthericum liliago*, St Bernard's Lily, dahlias and *Schizostylis coccinea* which do well in alkaline soils.

Agapanthus

The very name means 'flower of love'. At its peak, in July, the spherical head is packed with little trumpets, and, although it may be white, it is usually blue, varying from ink through lake and sky and smoke to Cambridge blue, like shifting seas in summer. Sometimes *Agapanthus* is mistaken for *Allium* because of the similar strap leaves, upright stems and balls of florets, but it is not a bulb, its roots being fleshy rhizomes. When finished, it fades gracefully – no mess at all – blue flowers changing to green seedpods, and in December fossilized to the colour of straw.

For agapathus in a border, plant the Headbourne hybrids, the toughest of the lot. These were bred in the 1950s by Lewis Palmer, then secretary of the Royal Horticultural Society, and are completely hardy, the only thing they need being sun. They even self-seed. They are never touched by late frost because they show the first leaf tips only in April. They can mix with other plants, but are supremely effective on their own.

Alliums

The onion family is ornamental and accommodating. The onions think nothing of surviving the driest summers in alkaline soils. They are companionable, growing with other plants, popping their globe heads over but never shoving others aside. They come up in spring, ease off white tissue caps, shake their hair out and look around. They may be tall and showy, or small and sweet. Dying beautifully is an art never glimpsed at the flower shows, but it is extremely useful to know how a flower fades. Will it be a dreary mass of brown paper balls or will it retain its skeletal elegance? Most Alliums pass the test with flying colours. Slugs cannot stand them, they are disease-free and their slim stems need no staking. They prefer full sun but can do well in dappled shade. With all these virtues, they can be forgiven for lacking scent.

The earliest to flower is *A. karataviense*, about 16cm high, with wide, grey leaves and powder-puff heads of pale mauve or white flowers. They die back and by July have vanished without trace. Later comes *A. cowanii*, which is perfectly pleasant but its white flowers are so similar to dandelion clocks one has to resist the urge to dig them out. *A. hollandicum* 'Purple Sensation' can be planted mixed with tulips, its varying shades giving colour when the tulips have faded. *A. christophii* in June is a big ball of mauve florets. It carries on for weeks, keeping its shape when the flowers are replaced by the green bubbles of seeds. It may be allowed to self-seed or picked and dried for flower arrangements.

A. carinatum subsp. *pulchellum* is small and graceful, about 20cm high and bearing deep rose bells on fine threads, giving a lacy effect. It also comes in white, and a yellow form is *A. flavum*. Pinks, mauves and whites are the usual shades of *Allium*, but an exception is *A. caeruleum* with little sky blue drumsticks about 20cm tall, and the sweet little yellow *A. moly* in June.

Allium include onions, shallots, leeks, chives and garlic, in flower all attractive and productive on dry alkaline soils. When leeks go to seed in their second year, the looping stalks and drumstick heads of flowers are shades of cream and mauve, buzzing with bees and perfect for drying. As for chives, with either mauve or the more uncommon white flowers,

ABOVE: Nectaroscordum siculum.

LEFT: Allium hollandicum *'Purple Sensation' with columbines.*

their grassy clumps are ideal for the front of a border where they are said to repel greenfly.

Closely related to *Allium* is *Nectaroscordum siculum,* often viewed at the Chelsea Flower Show with its subtle and exotic pink and green bells. It dies with little pointed seedheads, curiously bunched upwards, and has all the virtues of *Allium* growing in sun or shade, but can self-seed invasively and thus may need control.

The bulbs are planted in autumn, at about twice the depth of their length.

Anemones

Anemone blanda, with small, daisy-like flowers in March, will naturalize under trees, although it may take time to establish and several plantings before a colony becomes self-sufficient. Shades of blue are preferable to a mixture of white, blue and pink. The white stars of the wood anemone, *A. nemorosa,*

are perfect for an informal setting, and so is *A. n.* 'Robinsoniana', with pale blue flowers. Soak the tubers overnight before planting about 5cm deep. Other anemones such as varieties of *A. coronaria* are glamorous but less permanent.

Arum

Arum italicum 'Marmoratum', grown more for its wavy, arrowheaded leaves with dramatic creamy veins than its 'Lords and Ladies' spathe, grows anywhere, in sun or shade, and looks well grown with little daffodils and snowdrops. Plant the tubers about 10cm deep in the soil.

Camassia

Camassia leichtlinii, with its spikes of deep blue stars in May, is a useful filler when daffodils are finished as well as being beautiful in its own right. The white

Camassia leichtlinii.

Camassia leichtlinii *'Alba Plena'*.

double camassia, *C. leichtlinii* 'Alba Plena', has blooms like small tuberoses slightly later and gleams when grown in shade. *C. cusickii* 'Zwanenburg' has royal blue petals fading to azure at their centres. Camassia does not flop and needs no staking, all it requires is to be planted with the tops of its bulbs about 7–8cm from the surface of the soil, incorporating plenty of compost so that the bulbs do not dry out during the growing season. It looks best in groups of six, ten or more bulbs, it is happy in sun as well as shade and, as well as being fine in borders, can be naturalized in grass. It comes come from North America, where it was food for Indians who called it *quamash*, from which *Camassia* gets its name.

Chionodoxa

See **Scillas**.

Commelina tuberosa

This plant blooms through the second half of summer, producing small flowers of the most perfect deep blue pierced by two curling anthers. Its only disadvantage is that, being an early riser, it goes to sleep at lunchtime, and for the rest of the day its buds and flowers look as if they were dead. Although said to be tender, it can happily survive frosty winters under a mulch of gravel, emerging as late as May. Plant it using plenty of compost.

Arum italicum *'Marmoratum'*.

Convallaria majalis

'Lily-of-the-valley', with its evocative name, cool scent and white bells springing from the embrace of two leaves, is one of the sweetest, freshest plants of late spring. As so often, the common white type is better than the pink variety. *C. m.* 'Variegata', with fine yellow and white striped leaves is well worth growing. Although lily-of-the-valley should enjoy a cool, shady, moist spot, it has a will of its own and often wanders off to settle in full sun. Plenty of compost should be added when planting. When happy, it is useful as ground cover.

Crinum Lilies

Crinum powellii is a splendid, late summer attraction with large, fragrant trumpets. These are usually pink, but the white variety is particularly lovely. Its only disadvantage is that the broad, strap leaves can look rather messy, making it best in an informal setting. It is one of those plants which dislike root disturbance, a useful characteristic meaning that it does not require a regular lifting and dividing. It should be planted in late spring at about 20cm depth, with compost incorporated in the soil so that it never entirely dries out.

Crocosmia

Crocosmia × crocosmiiflora, usually called *Monbretia*, with dull orange flowers in the sun, is one of those flowers which should come with a word of warning. It spreads everywhere, in sun and shade, though it never gets to flowering anywhere that is too dark. However, its aristocratic relation, *C.* 'Lucifer', is fiery rich red, beautiful and, as the flowers fall off, they leave neat ladders of seed heads. A clump slowly increases. There is also *C.* 'Jenny Bloom', yellow. It blooms in late summer, and the corms are planted in early spring, in full sun, at about 7–8cm deep.

Crocus

With chalices holding ginger-tipped styles and yellow stamens and their bright delicate colouring, crocuses are the most welcome, earliest and easiest of winter plants. When it comes to choosing, the catalogue is yours – 'Mr Pickwick', white feathered with violet, 'Cream Beauty', 'Blue Pearl' and dozens more. Again, it is more effective to have a spread of a single colour or two complementing colours rather than a mixed bag of orange, white, blue, cream, purple and mauve, which gives a speckled result. They enjoy full sun, but will get sufficient under a deciduous tree.

For naturalizing, try *Crocus tommasinianus*, lavender with a silvery outside. This prefers semi-shade and, when settled, will seed everywhere, but not invasively. Other varieties of this crocus include the amethyst violet *C. tommasinianus* 'Barr's Purple'.

Crocus can be given a troublesome time from mice and squirrels, particularly the latter who dig up the corms leaving dusty depressions. If this occurs, plant more corms, about 4cm below the surface, and place a sheet of chicken wire over them and then the soil above. When planting in grass for naturalizing, this involves cutting and rolling back the turf, planting the corms and placing the chicken wire in position, and replacing the turf – all troublesome but worthwhile to ensure the corms' survival.

Cyclamen

The autumn *Cyclamen hederifolium* and *C. coum* arrive at the end of a dry August, dappling the ground pink or white under trees and shrubs. Both colours are good but, on soil where chalk lies like lumps of dirty salt, the strong pink, sometimes magenta, is preferable. Like snowdrops, they look marvellous as a group but also repay more intimate inspection. The brown balls of seedpods dangle from spiralling stems, the triangular leaves are delicately marbled and the flowers lay back their petals like the points of a crown. The fat corms, like small, round loaves – sowbread is one of their names – should be planted just below the surface, about 2 to 3cm, incorporating some leaf mould if available. If dry and wrinkled, the corms may be soaked overnight. Once established, they will increase in size, and self-seed in the most welcome manner. There are several varieties, including *C. coum* 'Pewter' with burnished leaves. *C. repandum* is the hardiest spring cyclamen but, although as lovely, it is not always so eager to increase.

Eranthis hyemalis

Under a tree in February the winter aconites can be a sheet of gold with little cup flowers, lightening the day. They can be grown with snowdrops but they may be hard to establish. If dry tubers are planted in autumn, first soak them overnight to let them swell, but ideally plant them green in March after flowering. However, even the latter method does not guarantee success, although it is worth persevering because, once settled, they continue indefinitely.

Erythroniums

The dog's tooth violet, *Erythronium dens-canis*, does brilliantly in shade in the lightest alkaline soil. The easiest to try, increasing generously, is the yellow *E. d.* 'Pagoda'. This can be naturalized in grass, the leaves whirling up in spring, followed by flowers. The grass should be left unmown for about six weeks after the tented flowers have collapsed. Although available dry from catalogues, the dog's tooth violet is best planted green. Once success has been achieved with *E. d.* 'Pagoda', try *E. d.* 'White Splendour'.

Eucomis

The pineapple lily, *Eucomis comosa*, has bottle brushes of whitish green flowers topped by green cockades in late summer. Like several other plants said to be tender, it will survive outside in a sheltered spot, particularly if given the protection of a mulch, because it is slow to get into action and never troubled by late frosts. Plant in spring, with the tips about 2cm from the soil surface.

Fritillaria

The nodding, chequered heads of snakeshead fritillaries, *Fritillaria meleagris*, subtly beautiful, are interspersed with an occasional albino, echoing the pattern in ghost form. To get them to naturalize, it may be necessary to plant and plant again, until they realize that they can continue on their own. They enjoy alkalinity, and although river meadows are their native habitat, they can naturalize on a dry hillside. They can be left to self-seed, but more rapid results are achieved if the seed is collected when ripe, placed on the surface of compost in a seed tray, watered and

Erythronium dens-canis *'Pagoda'*, *the dog's tooth violet.*

left in an open, shady place. Early the following spring, a mass of green threads will arise. These can be individually potted and planted out a year later when the bulbs are large enough to survive.

The glamorous 'Crown Imperial', *F. imperialis*, yellow, orange or red, was introduced from Turkey to the royal gardens of Vienna in 1576 and later to England. If one of the bells topped by a crown of green leaflets is tilted, drops of nectar like a crystal necklace are revealed at the base of each petal. They enjoy a well-fed, drained soil in full sun, and plenty of compost must be incorporated when planting. The bulbs have a depression at the top, and gardeners on heavy soils plant them sideways to prevent water from rotting the hollow.

Small fritillaries, such as *F. acmopetala*, pale green petals alternating with brown, need close inspection for their fine markings and interior life to be appreciated and may appear invisible against the soil. They show up better grown through pale gravel. *F. pyrenaica*, brown-maroon outer petals and a glistening, greeny-yellow interior, is happy in dry and shady conditions; in one garden it has survived and flowered for years under a catalpa tree. *F. pontica* too can take some shade. Other fritillaries enjoy sun. The shorter varieties can be planted 13cm deep and the 'Crown Imperials' at 45cm.

Snake's head fritillary, Fritillaria meleagris.

RIGHT: *Snowdrops in February.*

Galanthus

Snowdrops enjoy alkaline soils and in the garden they look best growing naturally, as a wandering path along the north side of a hedge or like snow under trees. In a rockery they can be grown in little drifts. In 1597 John Gerard wrote in his *Herball* that, although they have no medicinal use, 'they are maintained and cherished in gardens for the beauty and rareness of the flowers and the sweetness of their smell.' They dread full sun. Once settled, they naturally increase. Their propeller petals and fine, green-edged tube hanging from the hairlike stalk can only be appreciated close up, and galanthophiles, so passionate about snowdrops that they collect every available species, grow their collections in separate islands, taking care to avoid cross-pollination and subsequent hybridization. However, these islands lack the effect of a white carpet stretching under the trees.

Snowdrops, Galanthus nivalis.

The slim, single snowdrop *Galanthus nivalis* is lovelier than the double variety, *G. n.* 'Flore Pleno', bulging with petticoats. Both spread with ease. *G. plicatus* has dark green leaves with their edges turned under; *G. n. viridipice* has intriguing outer petals tipped with green; *G. ikariae* has bright green, glossy leaves; *G. caucasicus* has bold, grey leaves; *G. elwesii*, the Giant Snowdrop, is a native of Turkey. There are also named hybrids like the particularly handsome 'S. Arnott', which can be happy in full sun. The early variety *G. reginae-olgae* is usually in full flower at Christmas.

Snowdrops are untroubled by rabbits or squirrels and have virtually no pests. They are best planted green after flowering. If, after two or three years, there is no sign of increase, a clump can be teased apart after flowering and replanted with a dusting of bonemeal.

Galtonia

Galtonia candicans is imposing at the height of summer with its spires of white bells, and looks good planted in a group. It likes full sun and a well-drained soil, but in colder areas may succumb to frost. It helps to plant the bulbs deep, at about 18cm, and to give them a winter mulch of leaf mould.

Hemerocallis

Called 'day lilies' because each bloom only lasts a day, with their mass of buds they flower through July and into August. What they like is plenty of light. Their virtues are legion: they grow in clumps where weeds do not stand a chance, dying down in autumn and springing up their bright green spears in March or earlier; they are strong enough to need no staking, and never flop; they die neatly; they are happy in any soil, including alkaline; they appreciate dead heading and a winter feed, but can survive and bloom without attention and, in fact, can be left undisturbed for years.

If day lilies do have a problem, it is the colour. Some are brilliant red and orange, not always the easiest colours to accommodate, and a few years ago the main option was dusty orange, not that inspiring. However, these days there are a wealth of dark, almost black day lilies, and white and palest yellow as well as bicoloured. Some are fragrant, including the dainty yellow 'Nora', which flowers in June. Several have 'diamond dusting', a fine iridescent sparkle, caused by evaporation and making the petals glitter like jewellery.

They can be grown in a mixed border, but their exuberance may push shyer plants aside. They look well grown on their own in front of shrubs or shrub roses. Incorporate plenty of compost into the soil when planting them so that they never entirely dry out.

Hyacinthoides

No country boasts such bluebell woods as those in Britain. In early May the flowers extend like low misty seas and, with their delicate scent rising under bare trees mossy with the first signs of leaf, they create the environment of another world. The

Bluebell wood in May.

English bluebell is violet blue, scented, slim, with a folded, nodding head, and should be distinguished from the Spanish bluebell, which is usually on offer and said to be responsible, through hybridization, for contaminating the English bluebell. The Spanish bluebell is a lighter blue – it also comes in shades of pink and white – with larger flowers, a more upright stance and less scent, and can flourish in full sun. It is worth noting the difference. In catalogues the English bluebell has a plethora of Latin names, but these days it is usually *Hyacinthoides non-scripta*. The Spanish bluebell is *Hyacinthoides campanulata*.

Bluebells are best planted green. They can be grown under a group of trees or in an orchard. In one garden, not large, they are planted with clumps of male ferns under silver birches; the effect in May is ravishing. The plant requires little maintenance.

Hyacinthus

Hyacinths are usually planted in the autumn, but Christmas bulbs can be planted out after flowering. Most vigorous and with the best smell is *Hyacinthus orientalis* 'Delft Blue'.

Iris

Sun and more sun and a well-drained soil are what most irises need. The most reliable winter iris is *Iris unguicularis*, with three blue petals each marked by a white oval with stippled blue lines and a yellow path directing insects inside. The flowers emerge in spikes through the winter and are perfect for picking. They unfurl indoors, when outside they are usually blasted by frost. This iris likes shallow planting the base of a south-facing wall or fence is ideal. It is not for the

Iris unguicularis *likes shallow planting in a sheltered spot, where it will flower from late December.*

The May flowering *I. germanica* is the classic bearded iris portrayed in the fleur-de-lis of Boy Scouts and the Bourbon kings. The range of colours is so heavenly that the goddess of the rainbow could hardly have been named anything else. But, although the bearded iris likes limy soils and their drainage, it is not always easy to grow. The rhizomes should be laid, partly uncovered, in a shallow trough along the surface of the soil. If it fails to thrive, the problem may be a lack of sun – it needs at least six hours' sun a day. It is important that the rhizomes are not overshadowed by other plants, and are in a fairly low nutrient soil.

If success with the bearded iris is elusive, go for the more tolerant *I. sibirica*, slim and smaller, but coming in some beautiful colours. *I. sibirica* is often said to require a damp, rich soil but, in fact, it does well in a fairly dry situation. Just incorporate plenty of compost and water well when planting, and in a drought check that the soil has not dried out entirely (although alkaline soils rarely do deep beneath the surface). Excellent varieties are: *I. sibirica* 'Silver Edge', deep purple with a fine white rim; *I. s.* 'Soft Blue' and *I. s.* 'Creme Chantilly'. *I.* 'Holden Clough', yellow, finely striped maroon, takes a very dry soil and increases rapidly. *I. pallida* 'Variegata', with soft violet flowers is similar in its needs; its main feature is its beautiful leaves striped grey-green and silver.

tidy minded, because the blue spikes poke out of a jumble of half dead leaves. The plant can be given a manicure before flowering, or all leaves can be cut in summer to enforce new growth.

I. danfordiae and *I. reticulata* are trickier winter blooms, more reluctant to return year after year, and tending to split into a mass of non-flowering bulbs. Try planting them at least 8cm deep. Lifting and storing them after flowering may help.

Iris *'Holden Clough'.*

Fruit of Iris foetidissima; *this iris can take a dry and shady situation under trees.*

For the edge of a pond, try varieties of *I. ensata* which come in clear delicate colours. For a larger, informal pond, nothing compares with the native English flag, *I. pseudacorus*, with its tall, yellow flowers requiring no cosseting or protection at all.

The stinking iris (it is the smell of the roots) *I. foetidissima* is one of the best plants for dry shade, and has the plus of pods splitting to reveal shining, orange seeds in winter. The leaves are evergreen, and the intricate lacing on the summer flowers is intriguing although hardly noticeable at a distance. It frequently self-seeds.

Leucojum

These outsize cousins of snowdrops with fine green markings look wonderful springing up in small groups. They flower in early May. Like *Camassia*, they can be grown under deciduous trees, where, for most of the season, they sit in shade, but can also take sun. *Leucojum aestivum* 'Gravetye Giant' is the most handsome.

Lilium

When it comes to lilies on alkaline soil, impulse buying can turn out to be expensive. Some lilies (*Lilium martagon, L. regale, L. candidum, L. henryi* and their hybrids) enjoy alkaline soil, some (*L. davidii, L. pyrenaicum, L. longiflorum,* the Asiatic hybrids) tolerate it, while others (*L. speciosum, L. nepalense,* the Oriental hybrids) turn up their toes. A fuller list can be found in Appendix I.

Lilium martagon, the Turks cap lily, enjoys dappled shade. Its tiers of little petal bells curl up to reveal golden anthers and, when they fall, the stems stand like green candelabras holding seed, which in due course may be collected and sown. The usual type is an uninspiring, pinky mauve, but *L. martagon* 'Album' glows like little lamps in the shade.

Lilium martagon *'Album'*.

For full sun try the orange *L. henryi*, which appears year after year without trouble, bearing a mass of large, deliciously warty blooms with curling petals, often more than thirty on a single stem. Usually lilies do not need support, but here, if the weight of blooms drags it to the ground, the plant will require it.

Both *L. martagon* and *L. henryi* are unscented, which is why the white *L. regale* and its progeny are so precious, by day and night infusing the air with fragrance. These include 'Golden Splendour' and 'Pink Perfection', actually a rather beetroot pink; all can be grown in the sun or part shade. These lilies have generous trumpets holding a curling style ringed by massive ginger anthers like gnomes' suede bootees. If touched, the ginger pollen stains the face, hands or clothing. With this in mind, breeders have produced a series of 'safe', antherless lilies; they appeal to some. The slightly temperamental Madonna lily, *L. candidum*, is the oldest lily in cultivation and the one held by the archangel Gabriel in Renaissance paintings of the Annunciation. This lily should be planted as early as late August or September, since in autumn it sends up a ring of basal leaves which persist through the winter.

All lilies need good drainage. Most, including *L. henryi* and *L. regale*, sending out anchoring roots from the stem above the bulb, should be planted at a depth of about 15 to 20cm. A few with leaves springing at the base, including *L. candidum* and *L. martagon*, should be planted at a more shallow level, about 3 or 4cm from the soil surface. To avoid trouble from slugs, a little sharp sand may be placed at their base and above their tips. When planting, add some compost or leaf mould to the soil, but nothing too rich.

The lily's main pest is the lily beetle which produces a mass of sludge over the leaves and stems. It is easily recognizable, being a bright, lacquered red. If an infestation occurs, the lilies may be sprayed with Provado Ultimate Bug Killer, which provides protection for about six weeks. The beetles can also be evicted through regular inspection, being picked off and destroyed.

Muscari armeniacum

Although the grape hyacinth is a welcome fellow, few sing its praises because it lacks the glamour of tulips or the rarity of some fritillaries. It is a good companion in front of tulips and daffodils and, mingled with primulas, its blue bells with a hint of mauve, white rimmed, show them up but never take precedence. As well as blue, there is a white variety, *M. botryoides* 'Album'; the dull yellow but beautifully fragrant *M.*

Lilium regale.

Daffodils at Bramdean House, Hampshire.

BELOW: Narcissus *'Jenny' is excellent for naturalizing.*

macrocarpum; and the fluffy-headed, sterile *M. comosum* 'Plumosum'. It naturalizes easily, in sun or shade. Although spring flowering, the leaves usually appear the previous autumn and so it should be planted on arrival, usually in autumn, without delay. About 8cm deep is the best level.

Narcissus

Daffodils, spring staples of every garden, relish the English climate, the damp, muggy winters, the uncertain springs and summers. There is a wide range of sizes and colours, gold, pink, white and cream and dual-coloured combinations. Usually scented, they return without trouble year after year. They can take sun or dappled shade.

It seems only a question of asking which ones but, in fact, double varieties such as the messy 'Lion's Head', 'Golden Ducat' and little 'Rip van Winkel' like a dandelion are best avoided, because their heavy heads keel over, becoming food for slugs. In an exposed, windy situation, go for the smaller daffodils, like 'February Gold', fine and elegant, or the multi-headed 'Tête-à-Tête'. For brightness, try 'Jetfire' with its flaming trumpet. Under a pink cherry, choose a paler daffodil, such as 'Jenny' – a wonderful little naturalizer – or 'Thalia', which starts blooming a rich cream and fades to white. 'Jack Snipe' is a later white and excellent.

When grown in grass, daffodils look better in drifts rather than clumps. Any dreariness as they brown and bend is obviated by the contrast of adjoining grass scrupulously mown. Excellent gold daffodils are the classic 'King Alfred', 'Carlton' and 'Golden Harvest'. 'Spellbinder' is pale yellow with a white trumpet trimmed with yellow. 'Mount Hood' is the best of the large white daffodils, cream fading to white, and stunning in a drift. The orchid daffodils look exotic with their split and flattened trumpets; some gardeners dismiss them as freaks but, if found in the wild, they would cause a sensation and they are as reliable as the others. The yellow head of 'Cassata' is backed by a cream halo and 'Tricolet' has a flat, orange trumpet like a propeller.

The poet's narcissus, with its sweet perfume, comes later in May, and the best known is 'Pheasant Eye', white with its yellow cup rimmed green and red. Easy to grow, it is perfect for cutting.

There are several small species daffodils, for example, *Narcissus minimus*, informal and a tiny version of the Lent Lily, *N. pseudonarcissus*, which, with its laid-back habit and twisting petals, is best in a wild area. *N. triandus*, the Angel's Tears, with bending white flowers, is lovely and has the excellent 'Thalia' as one of its hybrids. Others can be tried, but some like the Hoop Petticoat, *N. bulbocodium*, really need a more acid soil to continue indefinitely.

Nectaroscordum siculum

See **Allium**.

Nerine Lilies

Another name for *Nerine bowdenii* is Naked Ladies, because the leaves come up and die back before the spidery flowers, shocking pink, open in October.

There is also a white flushed variety. They are welcome when the rest of the garden is finished and, in the cooler autumn weather, carry on for weeks. They are excellent as cut flowers. Plant them in a sheltered, sunny spot, incorporating some compost, with the tips of the bulbs nearly touching the surface of the soil. In this situation they will continue for years.

Ornithogalum

Star of Bethlehem, *Ornithogalum umbellatum*, opens its little, white petals in spring. *O. nutans* is sweet and elegant, each petal streaked with a green line. The bulbs can be planted in autumn, at about 5cm deep, in sun or shade.

Scillas and *Chionodoxa*

The squills and *Chionodoxa* are easy to establish and naturalize. The reason they are superior as small naturalizing bulbs is because in dull weather the blooms remain fully open, whereas anemones and crocuses need sun to expose themselves. Like so many bulbs, they look best en masse, and under a beech tree every March a thousand *Chionodoxa luciliae*, Glory of the Snow, become a lake reflecting the blue sky. The slightly smaller squill, *Scilla bifolia*, in a narrow border becomes a blue river. They can be

Chionodoxa luciliae
in March.

grown as small pools in rockeries or planted with dwarf narcissi, and Van Gogh might have been thinking of them mingled with little 'Tête-à-Tête' daffodils when he said that, where there is blue there should also be yellow. They self-seed and may pop up in adjoining lawns. The electric blue *S. sibirica* flowers slightly later, but, although lovely, is not so prolific nor suitable for naturalization. All the squills can be planted as bulbs in autumn.

Just one word of warning: avoid the pale pink scillas, which look grubby close to bleached alkaline soils; clear, strong colours are best. The little blue and white striped squill, *Pushkinia scilloides* var. *libanotica*, is charming held close to with its blue and white stripes, but insipid against the pasty hue of most alkaline soils.

Scilla peruviana – from the Mediterranean, not Peru – flowers some weeks later, with a violet pyramid of petals. It enjoys full sun and can take a dry site, but needs protection from slugs.

Sisyrinchium

The sword leaves of *Sisyrinchium striatum* are like those of an iris and of about the same height; it produces whorls of creamy flowers in early summer. Although attractive, it can self-seed extensively, particularly in the sun. More restrained and also self-seeding, but not with such enthusiasm, is Blue-eyed Grass, *S. angustifolium*, with little fans of leaves and bright blue flowers. It is perfect for small plantings in a rockery. Autumn is the usual time for planting the tubers, about 1 or 2cm deep.

Tulipa

Large tulips are best regarded as annuals. It is not that they object to chalk or limestone as such – they like the good drainage of most alkaline soils – but the home of most in central Asia has such a different climate, with harsh freezing winters and hot dry summers, that they rarely settle to giving regular appearances and, no matter how they are planted, usually dwindle to nothing after five years. In addition, they have been intensively hybridized for brilliance of colour without consideration of the morrow. If planted yearly, or every three years, they are easily grown and ready to flower. Lifting and stor-

ing after flowering and replanting in autumn helps to prolong their life. 'White Triumphator' is one of the most handsome and reliable.

Hope comes in the form of the little species tulips, several of which, given sun and good drainage, will continue year after year. *Tulipa turkestanica* is first to flower with wiry stems and pale little blooms in March. Later *T. humilis* 'Persian Pearl' is rosy pink with a green tint and effective at the front of a border. *T. batalinii* 'Bright Gem', bronze yellow, looks well grown with *Euphorbia polychroma*. *T. hageri* 'splendens' has up to five crimson blooms on a stem; *T. sylvestris*, a woodland native, can take some shade, and so surprisingly can *T. praestans* 'Fusilier', brilliant scarlet orange, splendid as patches of fire under deciduous trees where it can naturalize and carry on for years.

Tulip bulbs should be planted deeply, about 10 to 11cm down for the small ones, 16cm for the larger. They should be planted after other spring bulbs, in November; they are slow to get into action and if planted late have less chance of rotting in a soggy autumn.

Zantedeschia aethiopica

When it comes to the summer arum lilies, the one to grow is *Zantedeschia aethiopica* 'Crowborough', white, hardy and beautiful. One way of giving it increased protection and preventing it from drying out in summer is to plant it in a gravel garden and let the pebbles act as a mulch. It grows happily in a bog garden, but is more than happy in a drier site.

Zantedeschia aethiopica *'Crowborough', white arum lily.*

CHAPTER 7

Herbaceous Plants

It is possible to make a labour-saving garden with only shrubs and trees, but, oddly enough, the effect is not that inspiring. It has an institutional feel. A proper garden also needs small flowers, bulbs and perennials, and they do not necessarily require the hard work of heavy weeding, frequent division and staking. Major mistakes are made by planting trees and shrubs in the wrong place, but small flowers are easily shifted. Part of the charm of these flowers, browning and dying after the first hard frost, is their brevity, the way they live in the moment.

With so many excellent perennials, biennials and annuals enjoying life in alkaline soil, it seems best to mention those particularly at home, which are relatively trouble free, do not need staking and keep their looks into old age and beyond. Some plants prefer a lean rather than a fat diet, and on thin topsoil these are the ones to choose. Others such as peonies appreciate a rich feed when planted, but once established look after themselves. There are calcifuge perennials, and if planted they may give a decent showing for two or three years before retiring. Gypsophila, despite its name meaning 'lover of chalk', does not always flourish. It is, however, always worth trying a desired plant because many a well-nurtured flower has flourished in adverse circumstances.

Some plants on highly alkaline soils flower without the bright colours they show in more neutral habitats. The blue Himalayan poppy, *Meconopsis betonicifolia*, becomes a smudgy mauve, and the gentians which succeed in flowering are rarely true. Curiously, *Anchusa* and *Salvia patens* on alkaline soils produce stunning blues.

OPPOSITE PAGE:
Euphorbia characias
wulfenii *'Lambrook
Gold'*.

*Herbaceous borders at
Bramdean House,
Hampshire.*

SPRING AND EARLY SUMMER

Hellebores are one of the joys of early spring. Since their petals are not true petals but sepals evolved for toughness and protection, the flowers go on for months. The nectaries, which are the embryonic true petals like tiny flutes around the stamens, can be seen arrested at this precise moment of their evolution.

Perhaps the best known hellebore is *Helleborus niger* – *niger* referring to the blackness of its roots – the white Christmas Rose, but, in spite of its charming and spurious name, it has a tricky temperament. Better is *H. orientalis*, the Lenten Rose from the Middle East. It comes in a vast number of hybrids, white, green, red, blackest maroon, pink and particularly beautiful ones where the petals are dusted with sparks like firework explosions. There are also double hellebores with pointed petals in pompom style, surprisingly pretty and not laid low by the weight of petals.

In January the hellebore buds lie like fat pearls above the soil. In February and March they open carefully, tipping the heads slightly down to protect the exquisite petals. After giving their best for several weeks, the flowers die away neatly as the seed pods emerge.

Stinking hellebore, *H. foetidus*, is a chalk native with dark palm leaves and pea-green flowers like acorn cups rimmed red. Called 'setterwort', it was used for drawing out illnesses such as murrain, coughs and wheezing in cattle. *H. argutifolius* from Corsica is attractive with green flowers and jagged leaves with a silver film. *H.* × *sternii* has silver leaves and a mass of starry stamens.

Hellebores can be grown anywhere apart from in full sun. They are happy in well-drained soil under deciduous trees, and at the base of north-facing walls. Slugs do not seem to bother them, and they do not need heavy feeding. Once established, they resent disturbance or division, and the best way to acquire a collection is to buy good sized seedling plants in March when they are flowering. What you see is what you get: the habit, the way it presents itself, the markings and the colour and size of flower. Hellebores look good on their own, or growing with snowdrops or a ruddy grass such as *Carex comans*. If you want them to look especially trim when flowering, cut off the tatty, older leaves.

The University Botanic Garden at Oxford, with a pH of approximately 8.0 (alkaline indeed) holds a National Collection of *Euphorbia*. Mostly evergreen, they are excellent garden plants since their

Helleborus orientalis
seedling.

colour, coming from the flower bracts, carries on for weeks. *Euphorbia characias* subsp. *wulfenii* 'Lambrook Gold' is handsome, 1m high; in winter the upright stems hold their heads down, like birds tucking their heads under their wings, and then in spring they look up and become green-gold bottle brushes blooming above dark glaucous leaves. Like all the best flowers, it is not just handsome at a distance but exquisite in detail, the bracts holding flowers like little bell clappers. It can take full sun, but is happy in shade and, when the bracts turn brown, the stems can be cut at the base where fresh growth is already appearing. The deciduous *E. griffithii* 'Fireglow' is cheery with bright orange bracts spreading by runners, while *E.* × *martinii* has startling red eyes and *E. cyparissias* is low and ferny, with greeny-yellow summer flowers. The well-behaved *E. polychroma* has bright yellow flowers in spring, and *E. myrsinites* is like a large, spiky, blue-grey caterpillar. Similar to *E. myrsinites* but even better is *E. rigida*, larger, reliable, and flowering as early as January and February. *E. amygdalis* var. *robbiae* is useful as informal ground cover in shade. Most of these euphorbias self-seed but not invasively; the only ones which can spread too far are *E. griffithii* 'Fireglow', occasionally, and little *E. cyparissias*, much of the time.

Columbines are wonderful cottage plants, and it is fascinating to see varying shapes and colours interbreed and produce fresh forms all over the garden, in sun and shade, pleated, single, bonneted and bicoloured. Purists call columbines promiscuous, an inapposite word for such creativity. When *Aquilegia vulgaris* 'Norah Barlow', a mop-headed, pink and white columbine, seeds it can produce mop-headed children of rainbow colours. The disadvantage of self-seeding is that unpleasant colours, off whites, grubby pinks, mauves and cheerless maroons, need to be rogued out. For those who want a more refined columbine, the McKana hybrids, each a large butterfly of bright clear colours, are beautiful. They do not last indefinitely but are easily raised from seed.

In dry shade *Euphorbia amygdalies* var. *robbiae*, columbines, ivy, several ferns and honesty will do their best. The common honesty, *Lunaria annua*, is a purple biennial; the white variegated form *L. a.* 'Albavariegata' has ghostly, streaked leaves followed by glossy moon seedheads.

Aquilegia vulgaris *'Norah Barlow'*.

In late May and early June the peonies, rewarding plants with few pests or diseases, flower. They send out promising red shoots in spring. The earliest to flower are species such as *Paeonia mlokosewitschii* – called 'Molly the Witch' because of its unpronounceable name – soft yellow with a mass of gold stamens nestling pink styles and pinky, grey-green leaves. Later come the double flowers of *P. lactiflora* 'Sarah Bernhardt', apple-blossom pink and *P. l.* 'Duchesse de Nemours', double white. Both are opulent but perhaps the simpler beauty of *P. l.* 'White Wings', with single flowers surrounding golden stamens, is more lovely. In autumn the leaves produce good tints. Peonies take a year or two to settle down, but once established they should carry on in all their beauty for many years to come. They resent disturbance, which means that they never require the chore of division. No garden should be without its peonies.

Molly the Witch, Paeonia mlokosewitschii.

Peony 'Souvenir de Maxime Cornu'.

Crambe cordifolia is a tall, well-behaved plant holding a mass of little white flowers which turn into seedheads like tiny green marbles, and is ideal for the back of the border. If grown beside roses or other fragrant flowers the only disadvantage is its stale cabbage smell, hardly surprising since it is one of that family.

The fuzzy-leaved oriental poppies, *Papaver orientale*, are worth growing for their petals of crumpled tissue. They do not last long, but fall to reveal seedheads rimmed with fine velvet markings which, if

On the right, a cloud of Crambe cordifolia, *which later becomes a mass of little, green, marble seedheads.*

put in a box, would be mistaken for luxury choco-lates. Do not plant the ordinary, dull orange *P. ori-entale*, plant *P. o.* 'Patty's Plum', with subtle, bruised petals, *P. o.* 'Black and White', white with dark cen-tral blotches, and *P. o.* 'Marcus Perry', brilliant scar-let. These poppies, despite their splendid seedheads, do not die gracefully but flop around with browning leaves, and it is as well to have a chorus line like some late *Allium* or *Campanula* dancing in front when they are over. If you find no *P. o.* 'Patty's Plum' one year, and instead a mass of ordinary orange poppies, it has not reverted. Sometimes a good poppy dies from overcrowding by other plants, but sets seed of the plain *O. orientale*.

HIGH SUMMER

Great mullein and dark mullein, *Verbascum thapsus* and *V. nigra*, are natives that love it poor and dry, hot and sunny, and, although the great mullein is often covered by the black and yellow caterpillars of the mullein moth munching holes in the woolly leaves, they have good slug resistance. There are some lovely garden hybrids including a rainbow spread of *V. phoeniceum* varieties easily raised from seed. Good garden plants, they need no staking and give height in a sea of lower plants. There are also excellent species such as *V. spicatum*, with leaves hairy as if covered in cobwebs, and stately columns of creamy flowers. Given a sunny spot, they inter-breed and produce charming new seedlings.

Foxgloves have been called Fairy's Gloves, Fairy's Caps and Fairy Thimbles, and also Witches Gloves, Bloody Fingers and Dead Men's Bells because of their poisonous properties. Although usually found in acid soils, this biennial is happy in alkaline ones. They are brilliant garden plants because they never seem to be invasive but spring unnoticed until their spires dominate the surrounding flowers. Sutton's Excelsior hybrids have a colour range from white, through cream, primrose, creamy pink, rose-pink to deep pink and purple, and, once a colony is estab-lished, it may continue through self-seeding. To some extent it is a question of rain at the right time, and luck. Under dappled shade they have a pres-ence which can only be described as ethereal. If wanted, purple seedlings of the common foxglove

Papaver orientalis *'Patty's Plum'*.

Digitalis × mertonensis, *a sterile perennial foxglove.*

Digitalis purpurea can be rogued out at an early stage by removing plants with a purple staining on the back rib of the lower leaves. A subtle, sun-loving foxglove is *D. ferruginia* with tall spires of closely packed ginger flowers over a metre high. It often self-seeds.

A perennial foxglove enjoying sun is *D. lanata* with orchidlike flowers, each cream floret protruding a white lip. *D. lutea*, known for 400 years, soft yellow, about 0.5m in height, grows in sun or shade and its only requirement is well-drained soil.

The campanulas are wonderful summer flowers, but be careful about the colours. The widely available *Campanula lactiflora* 'Anna Loddon' looks distinctly grubby. Better is *C. l.* 'Prichard's Variety', with lovely spikes of deep blue flowers for three weeks or more. It may need to be staked in windy areas. *C. persicifolia* is another good bellflower, with delicate bells of white or blue and stems as fine as hairs. Another excellent, blue-flowered perennial is *Anchusa azurea*, and the variety to have is 'Loddon Royalist' with gentian blue flowers for weeks. It grows fairly true from seed. This member of the forget-me-not family likes the sun and has bristly leaves which repel predators. In an overrich soil it becomes moistly fat and may not survive the winter.

Related to campanulas and not widely enough grown is the balloon flower, *Platycodon grandiflorus*. Every year without fail it comes up, its buds swell like blue balloons and open into wide cups of flowers. Small, dainty and utterly reliable in any soil.

The cardoons, *Cynara cardunculus*, much like globe artichokes, are hardy in the southern counties, and look splendid in winter with their sheaves of young silver leaves. Growing to 2m they need space. Their buds, like spiky cannon balls, open into huge, blue thistle flowers, by which time the top-heavy plant usually keels over and is best cut down, when it produces fresh leaves at the base. The plume poppy, *Macleaya cordata*, with large leaves like jigsaw pieces and feathery orange-pink flowers, comes out in high summer when *Crambe cordifolia* is over, and, if space permits, is excellent at the back of a border. If happy, it spreads too far but its shallow roots are easily torn out.

In 1629 John Parkinson described over sixty wild and garden pinks. The flower seems to have given its name to the colour rather than the other way round, since pink originally meant jagged or fringed. To see and smell a vase of old pinks in June is breathtaking. The detail is as fine as a jewel's. Some are laced, others have a mottled or velvet texture with anthers like a butterfly's antennae, curling from the centre, all wreathed in a cloud of clove scent. Some of the best old pinks are: the laced

The cardoon, Cynara cardunculus, *in early March.*

'Dad's Favourite'; 'Musgrave's Pink', white with a pale green eye; and 'Paisley Gem', another laced pink raised by a Paisley muslin worker and presented to George III. Modern pinks are excellent and perpetual flowering, but usually without such a strong scent. 'Monica Wyatt' is an exception. Pinks like full sun in alkaline soil and are perfect in a sunny corner or at the front of a border. They get leggy after three years but are easily propagated from cuttings in summer.

The hardy cranesbill geraniums, so-called because the spiky seedheads resemble a crane's head and bill, are indispensable in any garden, and, since they grow as low mounds without strong structure, they look well with upright plants such as *Verbascum* or the most useful *Veronica spicata* nearby. They are trouble-free, unbothered by slugs, and they vary in their needs for sun and shade. *Geranium psilostemon*, magenta red with a black eye, forms a beautiful clump and will grow in any situation, *G. cinereum* 'Ballerina' is a little alpine with pink-veined petals enjoying the sun, while *G. pratense* 'Plenum violaceum' is studded with a mass of violet button flowers. *G. macrorrhizum* has aromatic leaves, little pink flowers and is useful as ground cover in shady spots. *G. pratense* 'Mrs Kendall Clark' is pale blue, with dark blue lines like the geometric patterns of rose windows in a cathedral. This fine patterning, in dark red on pink and in pink on white, can be seen on other geraniums such as *G. oxonianum* 'Walter's Gift' and *G. clarkei* 'Kashmir White'. With geraniums, as with pinks, the closer you get, the more you see. Absolutely excellent is a recent introduction *G.* 'Rozanne', which scrambles over other plants and flowers all summer with china blue blooms and a white centre. It prefers sun for only half a day. The sinister *G. phaeum*, the Mourning Widow, usually with blackish flowers, likes shade.

All the deadnettles like dry soils, but they can be dreary and one of the best, useful as shady ground cover, is *Lamium galeobdolon* 'Hermann's Pride', with leaves striped white and green and yellow flowers. *L. orvala* can take shade and has dusty red, large lipped flowers. For ground cover in sun, lamb's ears with its furry silver leaves is excellent; the best variety is *Stachys* 'Silver Carpet' because it rarely flowers and preserves its creeping texture without the need for clipping.

Macleaya cordata.

Dianthus *'Joan Siminson'*.

Phlomis fruticosa, *often classified as a shrub.*

Fuchsia magellanica *and* Artemesia canescens.

The silvery artemesias are excellent companions in a sunny mixed border, and the black-red, little flowers of the scabious *Knautia macedonica* are wonderful weaving through it. *Artemesia ludoviciana* 'Silver Queen' is simple and feathery, and *A. canescens* has fine leaves like curling filigree silver. In spring, cut back the artemesia to its first new shoots, otherwise it will get woody and die all too soon. Jerusalem sage, *Phlomis fruticosa*, with pale yellow flowers will also flourish in a hot, dry border, as will red and white valerian, *Centranthus ruber*.

Achilleas and hollyhocks lend a cottagey charm to a border, although *Achillea ptarmica* 'The Pearl' can be a pest, its thin, white roots sneaking everywhere. Stunning in full sun or in the shade, and perfect against a dark hedge, is white rosebay willowherb, *Chamerion angustifolium* 'Album'. It has white spires which turn into ladders of seedpods, becoming feathery later. It has a slight tendency to run, but is worth this breach of good manners. *C. a.* 'Stahl Rose' is a smaller, pretty pink willowherb, and, like the white variety, does not self-seed everywhere.

Two self-seeding annuals are worth growing. One is the well known love-in-a-mist, *Nigella damascena*, with feathery leaves and little, blue flowers cased in green filigree, and the other is the opium poppy, *Papaver somniferum*, source of heroin, morphine and laudanum, in gardens for centuries but doubtless if introduced today would soon be outlawed. Several varieties have depressing colours, but the single white *P. s.* 'Album' is utterly lovely with the sun shining through the translucent petals, and *P. s.* 'Pink Chiffon' is a cheery, salmon pink. If there seem to be too many shades of pink in the garden, black-red is a wonderful antidote, and among the opium poppies *P. s.* 'Black Peony' performs this function very well. When sowing it, the one essential is to keep the soil damp until the poppy seed has germinated, and, when it flowers, to rogue out any undesirable colours so that eventually you have only seedlings of the colour you want.

LATE SUMMER

When it comes to *Salvia*, forget those rows of pillar box annuals standing to attention in municipal displays. Grow *Salvia patens*, deepest blue, and *S. patens* 'Cambridge Blue', paler but as beautiful. These are not completely hardy and they can be lifted and put in a greenhouse for the winter, or cuttings are easily taken. *S. nemorosa* is the hardiest of these ornamental salvias, with dark amethyst spires in July. *S. sclarea*, clary or Clear Eye, which was used to dry perpetually weeping eyes, is a handsome biennial with white, pink or purple bracts, sometimes self-seeding;

Salvia sclarea *'Turkestanica'*.

its stuffy smell recalls the London tube on a hot August day. Painted sage, *S. horminum* (called clary, too) is an annual which comes in pink, purple-blue and white, and again the main colour is in the bracts which last a considerable time. Gerard in 1597 called it Wild Clary or Oculus Christi, saying, 'the seede put whole into the eies, clenseth and purgeth them exceelingly from waterish humours, rednesse, inflammation and divers other maladies', which one might imagine would only make matters worse. When the weather is warm, many salvias bloom with abandon until the frosts of autumn.

Phlox paniculata often develops mildew in dry soil, but the Springpearl varieties are modern hybrids which come in a good selection of colours and are more mildew-resistant.

The tree poppy, *Romneya coulteri*, is not hardy in all districts and not always easy to get established, but it is worth trying in a sheltered, sunny corner for its graceful, grey-green stems and leaves and the white flowers like tissue paper. Easier to establish for late summer are *Helenium* and *Rudbeckia* from the daisy family, particularly *Rudbeckia fulgida* 'Goldstum', yellow with a brown eye. It is essential to incorporate plenty of compost in the soil when planting it to prevent its drying out in a drought. Being sunflowers, all in bud follow the sun through the day, but by the time they flower the blooms are usually frozen in an easterly direction.

Japanese anemones grow to over 1m high and need no staking, and their flowers are one of the wonders of late summer. There are double and single forms, and pink and white shades, but the loveliest is the single white *Anemone japonica* 'Honorine Jobert', which has been in gardens since 1858. The only trouble about these anemones is that, once settled, they can become invasive, but any surplus is usually welcomed by friends.

Goat's rue, *Thalictrum*, grows easily and anywhere, but although amiable it is not an essential garden plant. *Thalictrum delavayi* 'Hewitt's Double', however, is. It can cope with dry soil, it likes sun, and has fine sprays of violet-mauve flowers nearly 1m high. *Lysimachia clethroides* is another beautiful perennial flowering from August onwards. It can take a very light soil, it never requires staking and, with its spires studded with white stars, grows to nearly the same height.

For butterflies in late summer, *Sedum spectabile* 'Autumn Joy' is necessary. Clouds of peacocks and tortoiseshells happily perch on the tweedy, pink flowers of this fleshy plant. If any increase is wanted, a few cut stems in water will produce roots within three weeks.

Michaelmas daisies are one of the last delights, giving a midsummer lift to autumn gardens. They flower away in soft pinks, reds, blues, creams and mauves. They are fairly shallow rooting and if too dry they may develop mildew, but the Italian starworts, *Aster amellus*, being more resistant, are best for thin, limy soils, which should be prepared with plenty of garden compost. Good varieties are: 'Sonia', soft pink; 'Vanity', blue-purple; and 'Lac de Genève', lavender blue. They may flop slightly, but should not need serious staking. *A. sedifolius* is also suitable and has fine foliage and starry flowers in August.

PLANTING AND MAINTENANCE

Autumn and spring are the traditional times for planting, although with container-grown plants it can be done at any time. In winter choose a mild day and in summer a rainy one rather than a drought. Soak the roots in water before planting with a spadeful of compost. In winter, spread any compost you can spare on the soil. Some gardeners swear by an annual mulch of bark chippings to maintain moisture

and keep down the weeds. Although an annual division and replanting of herbaceous plants is often recommended, it is not necessary until a clump displays smaller flowers and turns dead at its centre.

GRASSES AND BAMBOOS

Too many grasses in a garden give it a wild and scraggy look, lacking substance. But as long as they have sufficient room to sway and swing, among fleshier plants the grasses have a dancing quality. They nearly all do best in full sun. In late summer they are like clouds or fountains in a slight breeze. Left uncut in winter they look ravishing under frost.

The ornamental oats are splendid. *Stipa tenuissima* has wispy glumes like spun gold with the setting sun behind. *Stipa gigantea*, architectural, is like an explosion with its wands of fine glumes, but it has an occasional tendency to die at the roots. *Pennisetum alopecuroides*, fountain grass, has arching stems sprouting foxtails, the hairs tinged pink on the outer edge. *Miscanthus sinensis* is more upright, displaying silky cockades and growing to over 1m, and with careful placing develops as a striking late summer focus. *Carex oshimensis* 'Evergold' has bold, golden stripes, but perhaps the best all-rounder, not needing continual sun, giving a good show through the summer and dying down in the winter, is *Hakonechloa macra* 'Aureola', green and cream stripes growing in lax leaning clumps. It is excellent

Sedum spectabile *'Autumn Joy' covered by tortoiseshell butterflies and other insects in early September.*

for lightening up a shady area. All these grasses need minimal maintenance.

Festuca glauca and some other blue grasses such as *Elymus magellanicus* look fine for a season, but shabby the following spring, and take considerable combing and grooming before, if ever, they retrieve their looks.

Pampas grass is often dismissed, but its white banners must look glorious on the windy pampas of Argentina. It is a question of siting, because, even if growing well, a large plant looks cramped in a tight corner. *Cortaderia fulvida* from New Zealand is a fine pampas grass which can be a magnificent feature on its own or mixed with other plants in a border. *C. selloana* 'Pumila' is rather smaller.

Grow Gardener's Garters, *Phalaris arundinacea* 'Picta', but beware. It looks attractive in spring with striped white and grey-green leaves tinged pink, but its underground rhizomes creep everywhere. These are not too deep and can be pulled up fairly easily.

Some bamboos may be invasive, but a good, low one, well-behaved and enjoying shade, is *Pleioblastus variegatus* with gold and green leaves.

FERNS

Ferns evolved millions of years before the flowering plants and are among the most ancient plants. Their charm lies in their simplicity. The Christmas tree outline of a single fern is repeated in each frond and again in each pinnule, and again and again in a tripinnate frond where the outline becomes smaller and smaller. It moves from macrocosm to microcosm, all looking the same, yet none identical. In spring the crosiers are ecclesiastical as they unfurl from tight spirals. The spiral, symbol of growth and development – ammonites, snails, the buds of the forget-me-not family – is one of the earliest patterns used by mankind. Cool, free-draining and shady are the conditions ferns like. They are perfect in a dark corner beside a house, among rocks or on tree stumps.

Some ferns need acid soils to survive, but many are happy with alkalinity. The strappy hart's tongue, *Asplenium scolopendrium*, is a handsome chalk native which contrasts with other filigree ferns. The Rustyback fern, *A. ceterach*, is often found on shady old walls.

Path with grasses including Elymus magellanicus.

Fern uncoiling in spring.

If a fern arrives by chance, it is nearly always the deciduous male fern *Dryopteris filix-mas*, a good-looking beast. It is tall and upright and there are good varieties, like *D. f. cristata* 'Jackson' with curved crests, *D. affinis*, crested at the tips with green earrings, the bold *D. wallichiana*, and perhaps the best, *D. erythrosora*, with young growth coloured bright rust. All these can take fairly dry sites. The rather similar lady fern, *Athyrium felix-femina*, is no relation of the male fern and daintier in outline. If in doubt, look at the sori, the markings on the backs of the leaves which hold the spores. Those on the lady fern are little dashes and on the male fern are ringed. The Japanese painted fern, *A. niponicum* 'Pictum', is striking with its silver leaves but it is fussy and cannot stand a drought.

Some of the easiest, most beautiful and robust ferns for alkaline gardens, evergreen in mild winters, are the shield ferns. *Polystichum setiferum* from the Plumosum group has intricate spirals of densely arranged fronds and a slightly furry appearance; it is a lovely thing in dry shade. It is easily split for propagation and in spring all it needs is a tidying up. *P. munitum*, elegant and evergreen, can also take dry shade.

ALPINES

Stony ground is suitable for a rock garden, mimicking those limestone pavements where little plants cling to teaspoonfuls of soil and insert roots in every available cleft. Suitable plants include pinks, sedums, little campanulas, houseleeks, *Erodium*, *Draba* and Caucasian crosswort, *Phuopsis stylosa*, as well as herbs such as thyme and marjoram, and the little *Geranium* 'Ballerina'. *Parahebe*, like an aristocratic *Aubretia*, is easily grown, and so are saxifrage and small *Allium*. The low growing Maiden Pink, *Dianthus deltoides*, comes in varieties with speckled or deep crimson flowers. Edelweiss may be tried and, a winner, the creamy *Dryas octopetala*. These plants are best started well watered in a goodly pocket of gritty

Plants at the rock garden at Parcivall Hall, Yorkshire include Aciphylla glaucescens.

soil such as John Innes No.2. Autumn is a good time in which to get them settled before coping with the rigors of a dry summer, and the smaller the plant the easier it is to get it established.

WILD FLOWER MEADOWS

When it comes to wild flower meadows, whether in dry uplands or damper valleys, the assembly of flowers not only likes but needs poor, mean soil. This way, thuggish infiltrators such as docks and nettles have less space and food to colonize. Historically, the alkaline landscapes of the Sussex Downs, Salisbury Plain and the Yorkshire Dales were cropped by sheep, keeping the sward fine and permitting an amazing variety of small and undemanding plants. It is still possible to find over fifty different species in a single square metre. First come the primroses, cowslips and violets, then the yellow bird's-foot-trefoil and kidney vetch, and the white plates of yarrow, purple self-heal, numerous vetches, bloody cranesbill, wild mignonette, rock roses, scabious, hedge and lady's bedstraw, spotted orchids and helleborines, while in August there are harebells, pink centaury, salad burnet, the filigree outline of wild carrot and more.

To create a natural grassland you need a patch of ground in the sun, either bare or grassed. This can be a circular area within or at the back of a more formal lawn. Do not add fertilizer or organic matter, because this will feed the grass at the flowers' expense. If the ground is bare and moist you can scatter a lime meadow seed mix in spring, making sure until germination that it does not dry out. If you already have grass and a couple of wild plants, say daisies or cowslips that you want to increase, tease the clumps apart and grow the little plants for a couple of months in plug trays until their roots have filled out. Then replant them. Other plants may be individually raised from seed in the greenhouse and, when they are big enough to cope, planted in gaps in the grass. A rainy week and a pointed trowel are ideal for this.

The wildflower meadow can be restricted to natives or opened to other plants which can take the regime, such as crocuses, grape hyacinths and little daffodils. Taller plants can include *Geranium pratense*, ox-eye daisies, figwort and the wild daffodil. To keep

Wild flower garden with cowslips and spotted orchids.

the grass subdued, try growing yellow rattle, a semi-parasite. In a shady spot plants such as Solomon's Seal, snowdrops, foxgloves, wood anemones, blue-bells, lily-of-the-valley and honesty will flourish.

More exotic lime and chalk natives such as spotted and pyramid orchids, twayblades and white helleborine can be introduced, but their symbiotic relationships with specific fungi in the soil are intricate, and, although they may settle down, there is no certainty of increase. To some extent, it is a question of luck. The spotted orchid often arrives of its own accord on downland and stays. The marsh orchid can colonize chalky detritus from excavated lakes without the addition of any topsoil. In the wild flower meadow trim the grass when the plants have set seed, at any time from August or September. Remove the clippings to prevent their rotting and feeding the grass at the expense of other plants.

CHAPTER 8

Food and Herbs

THE KITCHEN GARDEN

The most productive kitchen gardens are those tilting to the south, absorbing the maximum of sunshine, warming early and cooling late. Not everyone has such a site. In a garden facing the sun but tilting northwards, there is summer sun but little in winter and crops must be sown later. In a shady garden with little summer sun, avoid vegetables such as peas and beans which involve flowering and fruiting and go for leaf crops, for instance, beet, spinach, lettuce and chard.

There are advantages growing vegetables in limy or chalky ground. There is no need to lime the soil. Cabbages are not going to suffer from club root. Many vegetables – asparagus, leeks, onions, cauliflower, kale, spinach, cabbage, in fact all the brassicas – produce well in soils of a pH up to 8.0. Other crops, such as celery, and particularly root crops, are more prolific with a lower pH.

On most lime and chalk soil little can be done in the long term to alter the basic pH of the soil, because of the presence of free chalk and lime particles, but an application of ammonium sulphate or flowers of sulphur helps to lower it for the season. More importantly, building up humus through manuring and composting improves fertility and ease of cultivation. Paths appear to sink as the enriched soil rises around them, and gardeners on alkaline soils who have worked their ground for years boast that there is no crop they are unable to grow.

Alkaline soils are frequently stony. Television gardeners sink spades into uncomplaining soil, but to dig an alkaline soil can be more like dentistry, easing and extracting stones with a fork. At first it seems that the primary crop is of stones, but, over the years, if larger surface stones are raked away and perhaps used as foundation for paths, the texture improves and stoniness decreases. The nurserywoman Marina Christopher considers that an alkaline soil produces the sweetest root vegetables, even if they are not perfectly shaped, and says stones are an advantage to the soil, improving drainage and stopping the soil from drying out. The installation of outdoor taps and water butts, helping to keep the soil moist during those crucial early stages of seed germination, should be included in the plans of every new kitchen garden.

Raised beds with planked sides, even if they are only 8cm (but ideally more) high, and filled with sifted soil will ease cultivation. They are ideal for all soils but particularly for limy clay which quickly compacts. They are easier to work, simple to tend, never get waterlogged, need never be trodden and to make them is an ancient practice. In the frontispiece of Gerard's *Herball* of 1597 a gardener digs while gentlefolk stroll round an arrangement of rectangular, raised beds. Order and control are the components of the kitchen garden and gardeners who wince at the gardens of Versailles are only too happy to discipline their own regiments of leeks and kale with never a wobbly line in sight. Ornamental potagers are fine as long as practicable, but the essential point of any fruit or vegetable must be its taste rather than its appearance in the garden.

Gardeners with new gardens on thin, hungry topsoil do not have as wide a choice as those whose soil has been worked for years. Here we shall mention only vegetables, including loose leaf crops such as spinach, spinach beet, lettuce and kale which perform in thin, dry conditions, and specific varieties which are less demanding. In the first few years of such gardens it is best to avoid broccoli, sprouts, cauliflower and cabbage, which prefer a relatively deep and moisture-retentive soil. The same goes for celery and celeriac.

Frontispiece of Gerard's Herball, *1597, showing garden with raised beds.*

BELOW: *Raised beds in the vegetable garden; in these every crop can be worked immediately after rain, without treading on the soil.*

Raised beds in late summer; the cages are used as protection from frosts as well as rabbits.

ROOT CROPS

When parsnips are required as perfect cones and carrots as long, fat truncheons, sow the seed in raised beds or sift the soil of each row clear of stones, allowing roots to dive straight. In stony ground Avonresister has short roots, resists canker and will put up a good performance anywhere. The ball-shaped carrot Lisa is good and quick to crop, and without the deep shoulder cavity typical of other round carrots. Parmex is another carrot with spherical roots and does well in stony soils where conventional carrots split and struggle.

When growing potatoes, go for scab-resistant varieties. For earlies, avoid 'Maris Bard'; 'Pentland Javelin' and 'Arran Pilot' have good resistance to scab and can take light soils. 'Foremost' produces an excellent crop in manured but unwatered dry, chalky soil. For second earlies, avoid 'Maris Peer', which fails in light soils which are not irrigated, and try 'Arran Banner'. For maincrop, 'Pentland Crown' is good, and so are 'Nicola' and the old 'Pink Fir Apple', with its irregular tubers and new potato flavour; both these last two are excellent for salads.

BEANS, PEAS AND LETTUCE

Broad beans are hardy, accommodating, resistant to slugs and pigeons and easy to grow in all soil conditions, even the dry and poor. They can be sown in autumn if the variety 'Aqualdulce' is used, or in early spring before the frosts are over; their taste when young is incomparable. The professionals dig a trench 60cm deep in March, manure it, cover and leave it, and a month later plant the seeds 15cm apart. Otherwise, dig in compost when and as you can, scatter on a handful of Growmore and plant the seeds. Broad beans are forgiving. If space is at a premium and the garden is exposed, try the 'Sutton', more compact than others. Or sow Thompson & Morgan's bean mixture with four varieties, separately named, in a single packet. Pinching out the tips discourages blackfly. If the beans suffer an infestation of blackfly a single blast of insecticide is sufficient to deal with them.

Climbing French beans, of which 'Blue Lake' is one of the best, are useful because they are easy to pick. Since they cannot take frost it is important not to sow until the soil feels warm to the hand, in late April or May.

Runner beans too, one of the most decorative vegetables, should not be sown until summer has come. In a small garden they can be grown up wigwams in the flower border, and, although the manuals say that they should be grown in different places from one year to the next, there are gardeners who have grown them satisfactorily year after year in the same patch. 'Hestia' is a mound-growing variety with red and white flowers which associates well with ornamentals. 'Desirée' is good in thin soils. The only essentials with beans are to water them in dry weather and to pick too soon rather than too late. Nothing is worse than stringy beans with coats of leather.

Peas require well-fed and cultivated soil, and in poorer conditions mangetout can be grown, because the pods are picked flat rather than bursting with peas. It is also worth growing the little asparagus pea – actually not a pea – with attractive, red flowers and little pods which can be cooked whole, about 25mm long.

On disadvantaged soils the loose-leaf lettuces give better results than the butterhead varieties, and have the advantage of regrowing after cutting. 'Lollo Rosso' is a deep red and crinkly, and grows well with the frilly green 'Funly'. If you are trying a cos-type lettuce, grow 'Corsair' which is sturdy, 'Little Gem' or varieties recommended for containers.

CHARD, BEET AND LEEKS

Beet Swiss chard is excellent, and the variety 'Bright Lights' has red, white or yellow stalks, delicious in stir fries, and its young leaves in salads. 'Lucullus', with white stems, is more prolific. If cut and left through the winter, it usually emerges as a spring crop. Spinach when young can be added to salads. Perpetual spinach – also known as spinach beet – although without the same delicate taste, is outstanding on thin, dry soils, being succulent, prolific and hardy, and virtually never running to seed in its first season.

Leeks are a joy to grow, but they do need a prior sowing in a nursery bed or tray and a later transferral to a main bed. When they have grown to pencil thickness, dig them up and take them to the main bed. Go along the ground with a dibber, making holes, drop a leek into each one and water. There is no need to firm the soil around them. If they are sown and left to mature in the same space, they will not be at a sufficiently low level for the stem base to thicken and whiten. 'Musselburgh Improved' and 'Toledo' are good varieties. On the ornamental front, if they are allowed to flower the following year, they produce beautiful *Allium* seedheads.

CUCUMBERS, MARROWS AND THEIR RELATIONS

When it comes to courgettes, outdoor cucumbers, pumpkins and squashes from the hot climes of America, they can take dry conditions and even neglect once their roots have sunk into hot, dry soil, preferably enriched with manure. Germinate and grow them on in the greenhouse, and, when the frosts are over and the soil is warm, plant them out, incorporating compost under each plant. With courgettes, the main necessity is to pick them as they appear, otherwise instead of scores there will be only a couple transformed to marrows. If a pile of manure is sitting in a sunny site, pumpkins will love the rich life riding on top.

PERENNIALS

When treated generously, perennial crops needing no disturbance come up every year offering their produce. No garden should be without rhubarb, easy and pest-free. Plant at least three crowns. 'Hawke's Champagne', 'Timperley Early' and the new 'Stockbridge Arrow', the last tender and stringless when forced, are good varieties. Plant in a sunny spot, incorporating compost or rotted manure in the soil. After a year the sticks will be ready for pulling. The most delicious rhubarb, with an exquisite colour, is forced. In January cover a clump with a forcer from Whichford Pottery – like a Buddhist temple, sculpture in its own right – and in March take off the top to reveal long, pink sticks, which can be pulled and need only the lightest steaming and a little sugar to taste like elixir of the gods. An inverted dustbin will do the job as well. If given an annual dressing of compost, rhubarb will produce more prolifically, but it is a good-natured plant, unlikely to die of neglect.

Ruby Swiss chard can be used as spinach, with the coloured stems chopped for stir fries.

It is a mystery why root or Jerusalem artichokes – the name comes from the Italian *girasole*, meaning sun follower and not Jerusalem – are not more widely grown. Ignore their reputation for inducing flatulence. They are useful for winter soup, and can be baked, mashed and roasted, they grow in most soils and carry on from one year to the next. Their knobbly lumps can make them fiddly in the kitchen and thus the smoother variety 'Fuseau' should be grown. When happy, they spread like weeds, and the roots are best grown in a separate bed or one lined at the sides with plastic bags to prevent colonization of adjacent spaces. A raised bed is ideal for this.

The roots of grated horseradish are so pungent that a mere whiff sends strong men reeling, but it makes an outstanding relish for roast beef, tastier than any bought variety. A coarse, ungainly plant, it grows in all soils and is another crop which can spread too far. It needs to be kept in a plastic-lined prison.

RASPBERRIES

Walking on chalk downs, escaped raspberries are seen, little groves with small but delicious fruit. They will grow anywhere as long as the soil is well drained, and, although they appreciate feeding and produce more prolifically with it, as with many crops lushness and disease can go hand in hand. Good varieties for the main season are 'Malling Jewel' and 'Glen Magna', but perhaps the best is 'Terri-Louise', bred by Medway Fruits. This crops in August and can be picked as late as December. It will then produce a second harvest the following summer. Dig holes for each plant, put in a spadeful of manure or compost – if not rotted, cover it with a little earth – place the roots of the raspberry on top and leave. In spring shoots will appear, which need to be tied to wires. In subsequent years apply another spadeful of compost or manure to each plant in early spring and cut the spent stems to the ground. The experts recommend the replanting of raspberries after ten years, but some gardeners boast of splendid crops from the same stock for nearly thirty years.

BLACKBERRIES

Blackberries are simple to grow. For huge fruit and ease of picking the thornless 'Adrienne' is good, and has a better flavour than 'Oregon Thornless', which, with its divided leaves and autumn colouring, is best as an ornamental. 'Fantasia' is prickly and prolific and has the subtle flavour of the wild blackberry. Blackberries will grow and fruit in a mound, along wires or on walls in any situation,

A fruit arbour with apples and blackberries at the centre of a kitchen garden. The white lumps in the soil are chalk.

but in shade the fruit is tarter than in the sun. Cut back the spent fruiting canes any time after picking ends and before growth starts in early spring.

GOOSEBERRIES AND BLACKCURRANTS

Gooseberries are more tolerant of dry alkaline conditions than most other soft fruit. They will grow in any aspect and in any soil, although composting and sun are appreciated. For ease of picking, half-standard gooseberries, about 60cm in height, are excellent and look splendid as sentinels on either side of the entrance to a potager or kitchen garden. As such, they take up less ground cover, since that below can be used by annuals. 'Careless' is a good cooking variety but needs prompt picking. 'Pax' is a new, spine-free variety which can be left to ripen into purple dessert fruit. 'Whinham's Industry' can be used for cooking when young or left to ripen into purple dessert fruit, fat as pullets' eggs.

When pruning, aim to create the shape of a vase. Cut the lateral shoots on the main branches to half their length at the end of June and again back to two or three buds in winter.

Blackcurrants, more demanding than gooseberries, need a richer soil. A good new variety, resistant

to mildew and the leaf-curling midge, is 'Ben Connan'.

STRAWBERRIES

Ken Muir, of Honeypot Farm in Essex, where he has spent a lifetime growing, showing and selling soft fruit, says that there are more than sixty varieties of strawberries in cultivation at present, but not all are worth growing. He recommends 'Elsanta' because of its proven record, and, to extend the season further, one could not do better than 'Florence' for cropping throughout the summer, and 'Mara des Bois' for fruiting in the autumn. These last two have excellent resistance to powdery mildew, and 'Mara des Bois' is 'perpetual', with the flavour of woodland strawberries. On light, alkaline soils, the strawberry bed should be watered only after flowering, not before. Never plant strawberries where potatoes have been grown because of the danger of transferring disease from one to the other.

GRAPES

The vineyards of France lie on limestone soils and alkaline gardens have no problem with grapes. The only necessity is to decide whether the vine is to be ornamental, or with some grapes suitable for wine making, or for eating. The most outstanding dessert grape is still 'Black Hamburgh', grown for centuries at Hampton Court and needing, like all dessert grapes, a greenhouse – unheated is fine – to produce its superb fruit in profusion. Plant the root outside, in a large hole with plenty of manure and compost incorporated (a horse's head is a traditional prerequisite) and lead the shoot inside through a hole at the base. This shoot can be tied to horizontal wires under the roof of the greenhouse and trained in a zigzag fashion to act as summer shading, while allowing full winter light when the leaves fall. When mature, after five years, allow it to produce about twenty-five bunches each year, cutting out the others. The traditional date for tidying up and pruning is Boxing Day. Pruning in February, March or April can cause death of the vine through the haemorrhaging of sap.

Outdoor vines can cover arbours and outdoor eating areas and produce good though sourer grapes, generally white and suitable for wine. 'Madeleine Sylvaner' and 'Mueller-Thurgau' are two good wine grapes, liking sunny positions. Avoid 'Siegerrebe' which is not so happy in alkaline conditions.

APPLES

Which is the best-tasting English apple? 'Cox's Orange Pippin' is the name that springs to mind. But this tree needs a rich, neutral soil as well as a host of chemical sprays to stay in good health. Far better, particularly for those without great depth of topsoil, to choose apple trees which are disease-resistant. Today few people want to spray tar wash, apply bands and the other prophylactics necessary to produce the ideal Aryan apple of supermarkets; many trees produce well, as they have in the past, without such attentions. Some of the best are old varieties such as 'Ashmead's Kernel', 'Egremont Russet', with its sandpapery skin, and 'James Grieve'. 'Fortune' is a good, early apple. 'Blenheim Orange' is still the best dual-purpose apple around, excellent for eating and in the kitchen. Good new varieties are 'Fiesta' and 'Sunset', both having 'Cox' as a parent, and 'Pixie'. There are also 'King of the Pippins' and 'Winston' as eaters and 'Grenadier' as a cooker. There is rarely need for more than one cooker, and the self-pollinating 'Crawley Beauty' is particularly recommended for thin, poor, chalk soils.

Take note of the rootstock the apples are grown on. M26 – called dwarfing – produces trees growing

Archway of apples, with Allium *and* Nepeta *below.*

to 2.5m, though in thin soils their height will be less. MM 106 – called confusingly semi-vigorous and semi-dwarfing in several catalogues – produces trees up to 3.6m high and is usually the rootstock of unlabelled apple trees in garden centres. Avoid the dwarfing rootstock of M9, which needs a rich soil to do well and on highly alkaline soils is unlikely to flourish. Most apple trees need pollinators, and a near neighbour's or an ornamental crab will perform this function as effectively as any other.

Tall, inherited apple trees tend to be cookers and are best regarded as ornamentals by all except the most agile. Renewal pruning, cutting out old branches and diseased growth, removing crossed and dead branches, is heavy work. Have them pruned by a professional, or leave them, with pink-shelled blossom in spring and a windfall of fruit in autumn. Or cut them down and plant other fruit trees in their place.

PEARS

Pears are more demanding than apples, needing a richer soil, but wonders can be achieved anywhere by planting well, with a hole far larger than the roots of the young tree about to go in, and by incorporating good matter. Pears come into flower earlier than apples, and, being susceptible to frosts, are best planted in a sheltered site. There is also the disadvantage that pears do not keep long. They should be picked when hard, left to ripen and eaten as soon as they are ready. 'Conference' is almost self-fertile and will not need a pollinating partner – although will fruit better if it does – but most of the others do. 'Beth' is a new variety not seen in the shops because of its fruit of varying size; it grows well in association with another new pear, 'Concorde', which boasts 'Doyenne du Comice' with its outstanding flavour as one of its parents. The self-fertile 'Durondeau' is compact, with little fruits storing comparatively well and turning fiery red in autumn.

CHERRIES

Growing cherries has been made easier by the introduction of self-fertile varieties, developed in Canada, through the grafting of sweet cherries to the new dwarfing rootstocks 'Gisela' and 'Tabel', producing small trees about 2m high. 'Celeste' is good for a small garden, and so is 'Cherokee', and both are better than 'Stella'. Like pears, cherries flower early and need a sheltered position.

PLUMS AND GAGES

The most popular plum is still 'Victoria', but as good if not better are 'Jubileum', introduced in 1999 with larger fruits, and 'Majorie's Seedling', which is excellent both as a dessert and for cooking. 'Oullin's Golden Gage' is large, round, healthy and self-fertile. These are usually grafted on St. Julien 'A' rootstock, which makes them suitable as small trees or fans in less fertile soils. Few plum trees survive in high productivity more than twenty years.

QUINCES AND MEDLARS

Quinces and medlars are not only attractive with their dog rose-type blossom, but appeal simply because they have been grown for hundreds of years. The golden fruit of the quince can be made into jelly, and the strange crowned fruit of the medlar, subject of bawdy as 'dog's arse', can be left until it is 'bletted' – nearly rotten – before being eaten. The medlar can produce fruit in a shady spot, and both can live for years.

FIGS

No fig flowers are ever seen since they are enclosed within the fruit, but the fig is an attractive wall shrub with its large, trilobed leaves mimicking the outline of male genitalia and traditionally carved to clothe nude statues. Coming from subtropical climes, figs need a sunny wall to crop outdoors in Britain. To keep the tree compact and fruitful, root restriction should be provided, with the roots planted in an open-based box or through a square of buried bricks. On stony ground this necessary restriction may be provided by the stones themselves. Pea-sized embryo figs are formed in late summer and ripen into fruit the following summer, unless frozen off by a severe winter. It enjoys alkaline soil, and the most reliable and widely grown variety is 'Brown Turkey'. For propagation, layerings are readily taken.

COBNUTS AND FILBERTS

These closely related species of the hazelnut, a chalk and lime native, are wind-pollinated and two varieties are needed to ensure good cross-pollination. Cobnuts and filberts have a similar appearance; the difference is that the husk of the cobnut does not completely cover the nut, whereas the filbert's does. The most serious pest is the squirrel, which can steal a crop in a single night. 'Red Filbert', with claret-coloured catkins looks splendid growing beside 'Cosford' or 'Kentish Cob', with yellow catkins and green leaves.

PLANTING

All fruit trees should be planted in large holes filled with compost and manure – and kept watered in dry spells until they can cope on their own. Keep the ground around them weed-free until they are established.

HERBS

Many herbs relish impoverished, alkaline soils, performing better there than in luxury conditions where they keel over from an excess of fat living. The best leaf flavour comes before flowering when the plant's energy takes a different direction. Some, such as rosemary and lavender, are grown as ornamentals, but many are essential in the kitchen.

POT HERBS

Thyme and marjoram are pot herbs, adding flavour to casseroles and terrines. The name thyme comes from the Greek *thymus*, 'to burn a sacrifice', and in the Middle Ages a posy of aromatic herbs including thyme warded off the germs of sick people. The basic garden thyme *Thymus vulgaris* has a lemon-scented sister *T. × citriodorus*, and has spawned decorative varieties such as the variegated *T. citriodorus* 'Silver Queen' and *T.* 'Doone Valley'. The trouble about thyme is its inevitable legginess after a year or so, when, instead of remaining a tidy bush, it becomes gawky with leaves and flowers at the tips of the shoots. Then it can be drop pruned, which means digging it up, deepening the hole it comes from and replanting it about 8cm lower,

Golden marjoram and other plants in cracks along paving.

burying the legginess. Or cuttings can be taken. Free from this problem is creeping thyme, *T. serpyllum*, which may be white, pink, purple or woolly, and the sweetest *T. minimus*, a thyme for a doll's house or a cushion in the garden and perfectly hardy too. All these are attractive to bees and have a good flavour, although not as pungent as that of *T. vulgaris*.

Ordinary marjoram or oregano, *Oregano vulgare*, is so happy on dry chalk soils it can become invasive. Bees like it and the smell is strong, but perhaps a better choice is golden marjoram, *M. vulgare* 'Curly Gold', which keeps to itself as a low spreading and very pretty mat which persists over the years. The sweetest smell, better for pot-pourri than cooking, comes from knotted or sweet marjoram, *O. majorana*, so called from the little buds like knots along its stem. This is not hardy.

SAGE

Sage is another useful herb, and its Latin name *Salvia officinalis*, derived from *salvus* meaning safe, well, sound, reflects its use for ailments so numerous that one starts to doubt its efficacy. In the kitchen it is still a wonderfully dry counternote to the richness of pork with crackling and of goose. Like all silver-leaved plants, sage enjoys a hot, dry

situation and it can flourish in stony soil. It may get leggy and etiolated, and, to avoid this, cut it back in spring to just above the points of new growth. As well as the basic sage, there are ornamental varieties such as *S. o. icterina* with gold and green leaves, and *S. o. purpurescens*. A beautiful sage, with excellent flavour, is the compact *S. o.* 'Berggarten', with large oval leaves dusted with diamonds by the morning dew. Cut back each spring, it makes a soft silver mound in summer and through the winter.

FINES HERBES

Parsley, chives, tarragon and chervil are the classic *fines herbes*, with delicate flavours ideal for omelettes. They are best sprinkled fresh on food, rather than cooked.

Parsley can take some shade and enjoys a richer soil than most other herbs. Its lively green when freshly chopped makes it a kitchen essential, perking up the look of kedgerees, soups and all manner of pallid dishes. It has been used for centuries as a diuretic and to cure numerous ailments. Best for flavour is flat French parsley, and most glamorous as garnish is a curled or moss variety, which Gerard described as, 'admirablie crisped or curled like fannes of curled feathers.' Good Friday is the traditional day for sowing parsley, but it can be sown

Sage and cotton lavender.

Golden variegated sage, Salvia officinalis *'Icterina'; in places the sage has reverted to a more vigorous plain green which will have to be cut out if it is to maintain its variegation.*

until July in colder areas and August in warmer places. It is slow to germinate, taking about twenty days. To speed germination, make a shallow drill in the soil about a 1cm deep, sprinkle in the seed thinly and then pour water, as near boiling as possible, over it. For a good winter supply, it needs to be well established before the nights draw in and, although hardy, a cloche during severe frosts ensures a continual supply of green and upright sprigs.

Chives, hardy and perennial, belong to the alkaline-loving *Allium* family and have a milder flavour than their onion relative. It shows fresh green hair in spring and later mauve tufts of flowers, attractive anywhere. Some gardeners grow clumps along the front of rose beds to repel greenfly and lessen blackspot. It grows in sun or shade, in dry or damp soils, and for increase, divide it in autumn or spring.

Chervil has a delicate flavour for sauces and chicken dishes. It is an annual and, once grown and allowed to seed, its lacy leaves usually reappear the following year. It is well-mannered and never invasive.

When it comes to tarragon, the variety to get is French tarragon not Russian, which has an inferior flavour. When buying, avoid any label marked simply 'tarragon' because it will probably be Russian. It needs a sunny spot and, although a perennial spreading by tubers, it is tender, needing winter protection. The name tarragon is a corruption of the Arabic *tarkhun*, 'little dragon' and reflects the belief that it cures the bites of venomous beasts and mad dogs.

MINT

Mint grows anywhere, shade or sun, and, since it appreciates a richer soil, dig in compost when planting. The Romans used it for cleaning teeth, a taste continued in today's mint-flavoured toothpastes, mouth fresheners and chewing gum. For flavour, spearmint – so called because of the shape of its leaves – and the darker peppermint are excellent. So is apple mint, and the giant, slightly furry Bowles apple mint has a good flavour for mint sauce and jelly. Variegated ginger mint, gold and green, variegated pineapple mint, white and green, crested mint, with each leaf edge crimped and curled, are decorative and fun in a mint collection. Creeping pennyroyal, also called Cunningham mint, will provide a fragrant note underfoot and is hardier than the little Corsican mint with its tiny flowers. Eau de Cologne mint, *Mentha citrata*, has a heavenly smell when crushed, and can be grown to mask something smelling less pleasant, say a dustbin. Nearly all the mints are vigorous, best grown on their own or beside robust plants of similar constitution. If rust occurs on the leaves, pull the plant out and grow a fresh variety.

Winter savory, Satureja Montana, *is a perennial herb which does well on poor soils and bears attractive, little lipped flowers in late summer.*

SAVOURY, DILL AND FENNEL

The savouries are easy to grow and have an excellent flavour, particularly good sprinkled over broad beans. Plenty of sun and poor soil are all they need. Summer savoury is annual, while winter savoury is perennial and makes a neat, ornamental bush with little, white-lipped flowers in late summer.

Bronze fennel in spring, with fluffy growth.

RIGHT: *Bronze fennel flowering in August, with tired, old leaves stripped off to give a bamboo effect.*

Dill, a feathery annual, is a traditional accompaniment of fish in Scandinavian countries. It can hybridize with fennel, its near relation and a perennial also used in fish dishes. The foamy mounds of fennel leaves, bronze or green, enhance any flower border. It looks attractive early in the season, but by July as the flat, yellow, umbel flowers open, the leaves look desiccated. Then the plant can be cut to within a few centimetres of the ground, fed and watered, to produce yet more charming young growth. Alternatively, the leaves can be stripped off with the flower heads left, and the plant turned into a mini bamboo grove.

SWEET CICELEY, LEMON BALM AND LOVAGE

Sweet Ciceley, a perennial with ferny leaves, umbrella flowers and black seed pods was traditionally used as a sweetener. The leaves, with their liquorice taste, can be used instead of sugar to relieve the tartness of apple pie. It does not spread, but comes up in a small clump each year.

Golden variegated lemon balm, Melissa officinalis, *is less invasive than the common type.*

BELOW RIGHT: Angelica archangelica *is the herb of the archangel Michael, and with its fragrant flowers was thought to cure vast numbers of complaints. A biennial, often self sowing, its architectural presence looks well at the back of a border and/or against dark backgrounds.*

Lemon balm, *Melissa officinalis*, despite its pleasant citrus taste and scent and use as a infusion, spreads unmercifully, and here variegated golden lemon balm, *M.o. aurea*, has an equally good smell and is far better mannered than its gross sister. It will, however, produce seedlings of the common sort, which should be rogued out. The sharpest, best and strongest lemon smell comes from the pointed leaves of lemon verbena, *Aloysia triphylla*, from South America. This is tender and must be taken inside to survive the winter.

Many herbs come from the umbellifereae family, including parsley, sweet Ciceley, chervil, dill, angelica and fennel, and a handsome one, not widely grown, is lovage, with celery-scented leaves useful in potato soup and for sprinkling over salads. Traditionally grown as a love potion, it is a tall perennial, growing to about 2m, healthy and never invasive.

ORNAMENTAL HERBS

It is satisfying to grow herbs no longer widely used as food or medicine. Angelica, its stalks still crystallized for cake decoration, is a biennial with pale green, soapy-smelling flowers which can look magnificent at the back of a border. So can true valerian, *Valeriana officinalis*, which, with its pinnate leaves and pinky-white fragrant flowers, is taller and more elegant than the unrelated red valerian, *Centranthus*

ruber. Hyssop is a small, shrubby perennial with charming blue flowers which can be used as edging. For centuries it was used for purification – *Psalms* 51, 7: 'Purge me with hyssop and I shall be clean.'

Plants Recommended for Alkaline Soils

These lists are not exhaustive, being essentially the recommendations in the text.

> KEY: Award of Garden Merit from the Royal Horticultural Society: **GM**
> Denotes that all species and cultivars are lime-tolerant: **ALL**
> Denotes that plant succeeds in shallow topsoil: **ST**

TREES

Tall Trees

Acer platanoides 'Drummondii' **GM ST**

A. pseudoplatanus – sycamore **ST**

A. p. 'Leopoldii' **GM**

Aesculus hippocastanum – horse chestnut **GM ALL ST**

A. indica – Indian chestnut **ST**

Ailanthus altissima – tree of Heaven **GM**

Betula pendula – silver birch **ST**

Carya cordiformis – hickory/bitternut

Catalpa bignonioides – Indian bean tree **GM ST**

Davidia involucrata – pocket handkerchief tree, dove tree **GM ST**

Fagus sylvatica – beech **GM ALL ST**

F. s. var. *heterophylla* 'Aspleniifolia' – fern- or cut-leaved beech **GM ST**

F. s. 'Riversii' – copper beech **GM ST**

F. s. 'Rohanii' – cut-leaved copper beech **ST**

Fraxinus excelsior – common ash **GM ALL ST**

F. e. 'Pendula' – weeping ash **GM ST**

F. ornus – manna ash **GM**

Juglans nigra – black walnut **GM ALL ST**

J. n. 'Lacinata' – cut-leaved walnut **ST**

J. regia 'Broadview' – walnut **ST**

Liriodendron tulipifera – tulip tree **GM**

Populus × *jackii* – balm of Gilead

P. balsamifera – balsam polar

Robinia pseudoacacia – false acacia **GM ST**

Salix babylonica – weeping willow

Tilia × *euchlora* – Crimean lime **GM ST**

Zelkova carpinifolia – Zelkova elm

Medium and Small Trees

Acer griseum – paperbark maple **GM**

A. negundo var. *violaceum* – box elder **GM**

A. pseudoplatanus 'Brilliantissimum' **GM ST**

A. saccharinum – silver maple

Aesculus pavia – red buckeye **ST**

Alnus glutinosa – alder

Amelanchier lamarckii – snowy mespilus **GM ST**

Betula utilis var. *jacquemontii* – Himalayan birch

Buxus sempervirens 'Greenpeace' – box (columnar) **ST**

Carpinus betulus – hornbeam **GM ST**

Catalpa bignonioides 'Aurea' – golden Indian bean tree **GM ST**

Cercis siliquastrum – Judas tree **GM ST**

C. s. f. albida – white Judas tree **ST**

Cornus controversa – wedding cake tree **ST**

Crataegus crus-galli – cockspur thorn **ALL ST**

C. laevigata 'Crimson Cloud' – hawthorn **ST**

C. l. 'Paul's Scarlet' – hawthorn **GM ST**

OPPOSITE PAGE:
Syringa persica.

C. persimilis 'Prunifolia' GM ST
Carpinus betulus – hornbeam GM ALL ST
Eucalyptus dalrympleana GM ST
E. parvifolia GM ST
Gleditsia triacanthos 'Sunburst' – honey locust GM ST
Koelreuteria paniculata – golden rain tree GM
Laburnum × *watereri* ST
L. alpinum ST
Malus floribunda – crab apple GM ALL
M. 'John Downie' – crab apple GM ST
M. × *purpurea* 'Royalty' – purple-leaved crab apple
M. × *zumi* var. *calocarpa* 'Golden Hornet' – crab apple
Morus nigra – black mulberry
Paulonia tomentosa – foxglove tree
Prunus cerasifera 'Pissardii' – purple-leaved cherry ST
P. lusitanica – Portuguese laurel GM ST
P. padus – bird cherry ST
P. sargentii ST
P. serrula – Tibetan cherry GM ST
P. × *subhirtella* 'Autumnalis' – winter flowering cherry
Ptelea trifoliata – hop tree GM ST
Pyrus salicifolia 'Pendula' – willow-leaved pear GM ST
Quercus cerris – Turkey oak
Q. ilex – holm oak
Robinia pseudoacacia 'Frisia' – false acacia ST
R. p. 'Umbraculifera' – mop-head acacia ST
Salix purpurea 'Pendula' – weeping willow (small) GM
Sorbus aria – whitebeam ST
S. aucuparia – rowan
S. a. hupehensis

Conifers

Cedrus atlantica Glauca group – Atlantic cedar GM ALL ST
C. deodara GM
C. libani – cedar of Lebanon GM
Cupressus sempervirens Stricta group – cypress GM ST
Gingko biloba – maidenhair tree GM ST
Juniperus scopulorum 'Skyrocket' juniper ALL ST

Larix decidua – larch GM
Metasequoia glyptostroboides – dawn redwood
Picea glauca var. *albertiana* 'Conica'
P. likiangensis
Pinus bungeana
P. mugo – mountain pine ST
P. nigra – Aleppo pine GM
P. sylvestris – Scots pine GM
Sequoiadendron giganteum – wellingtonia GM
Taxodium distichum – swamp cypress
Taxus baccata – yew GM ALL ST
T. b. 'Fastigiata' – Irish yew (columnar) ST
Thuja plicata – western red cedar ST

SHRUBS

HEIGHT: T = TALL, M = MEDIUM, S = SMALL

Winter Shrubs

Chimonanthus praecox T – wintersweet
Cornus alba 'Sibirica' S
Cornus mas T – cornelian cherry ST
Coronilla glauca 'Citrina' S ST
Daphne bholua S/M
Lonicera fragrantissima M/T – winter flowering honeysuckle ALL ST
L. × *purpusii* M – winter flowering honeysuckle ST
Mahonia aquifolium M ALL ST
Mahonia × *media* 'Charity' T GM ST
M. × *m.* 'Underway' M GM ST
M. × *m.* 'Winter Sun' M GM ST
Rubus cockburnianus S – white-stemmed bramble GM ALL ST
Sarcoccoca hookeriana var. *digyna* S – Christmas box ALL ST
S. h. var. *humilis* S – Christmas box ST
Viburnum × *bodnantense* T ALL ST
V. × *b.* 'Dawn' GM ST
V. × *b.* 'Deben' T GM ST
V. tinus 'French White' T – laurestinus ST
V. t. 'Gwenllian' T – laurestinus GM ST

Shrubs for Leaves

Berberis thunbergii 'Aurea' M ALL ST
B. t. 'Atropurpurea Superba' M
B. t. 'Harlequin' M

Cercis canadensis 'Forest Pansy' M GM ST

Choisya ternata 'Sundance' S GM ST

Cornus controversa 'Variegata' T – wedding cake tree

Corylus avellana 'Aurea' M – golden hazel ALL

Cotinus coggygria T – smoke bush GM ALL ST

C. 'Royal Purple' T – purple smoke bush GM ST

Elaeagnus angustifolia T ST

E. 'Quicksilver' ST

Euonymus fortunei 'Emerald 'n' Gold' S GM ALL ST

E. f. 'Silver Queen' S GM ST

Fatsia japonica M

Ilex aquifolium T – holly GM ST

I. a. 'Argentea Marginata' M GM ST

I. a. 'Golden Queen' M GM ST

I. a. 'Ferox Argentea' M GM ST

Lonicera nitida 'Baggesen's Gold' S GM ALL ST

Osmanthus heterophyllus M ST

Philadelphus coronarius 'Aureus' M ST

Phormium tenax 'Purpureum' M ALL ST

Photinia × fraseri 'Red Robin' M GM ST

P. davidiana T ST

Pittosporum 'Garnettii' S GM

P. tenuifolium S GM

P. t. 'Purpureum' S

Rhamnus alaternus 'Argenteovariegata' T – variegated buckthorn ST

Rhus typhina 'Dissecta' M – cut-leaved stag's horn sumach ALL ST

Ribes sanguineum 'Brocklebankii' M ALL ST

Sambucus nigra 'Black Beauty' = 'Gerda' M elder ALL ST

S. n. 'Black Lace' M ST

S. racemosa 'Plumosa Aurea' M ST

Spiraea japonica 'Gold Flame' S GM ST

Symphoricarpos orbiculatus 'Foliis Variegatis' M – variegated snowberry ALL ST

Yucca filamentosa S – Adam's needle GM

Y. gloriosa M GM

Shrubs for Scented Summer Flowers

Abelia × grandiflora M GM

Buddleja alternifolia T GM ALL ST

B. davidii 'Dark Knight' M – butterfly bush GM ST

B. globosa T GM ST

Calycanthus floridus S/M – allspice GM

Carpenteria californica M

Choisya ternata S/M – Mexican orange blossom GM ST

Cistus ladanifer S/M GM ALL ST

Colletia hystrix M

Daphne × burkwoodii S

D. mezereum S ST

D. odora 'Aureomarginata' S

Lavandula angustifolia S – English lavender ALL ST

L. a. 'Hidcote' S GM ST

L. a. 'Twickel Purple' S ST

L. stoechas S – French lavender GM ST

Myrtus communis subsp. *tarentina* S – myrtle GM ST

Osmanthus delavayi M/T GM

Perovskia atriplicifolia 'Blue Spire' S – Russian sage GM ST

Philadelphus 'Beauclerk' T – mock orange GM ST

P. 'Manteau d'Hermine' S GM ST

Poncirus trifoliata S – Japanese bitter orange ST

Prostanthera rotundifolia S – Australian mint ST

Ribes odoratum M – golden currant

R. sanguineum M – flowering currant ALL ST

R. s. 'Pulborough Scarlet' M ST

R. s. 'Tydeman's White' M – white flowering currant ST

Rosmarinus officinalis S – rosemary ALL ST

R. o. 'Severn Sea' S GM ST

Spartium junceum M – Spanish broom GM ST

Syringa × persica S/M – Persian lilac GM ALL

S. velutina M ST

S. vulgaris 'Souvenir de Louis Spaeth' T – lilac ALL ST

S. v. 'Primrose' M/T ST

Viburnum × burkwoodii 'Anne Russell' M GM ALL ST

V. carlesii M ST

More Shrubs for Summer Flowers

Abutilon × suntense 'Jermyns' T ST

Caryopteris × clandonensis 'Arthur Simmonds' S GM ALL ST

Ceanothus 'Gloire de Versailles' T GM ALL

C. 'Puget Blue' M GM

C. arboreus T

C. thyrsiflorus 'Millerton Point' M ST

Ceratostigma willmottianum S – shrubby plumbago GM

Colutea arborescens T – bladder senna ST

Cornus kousa var. *chinensis* M/T – flowering dogwood `GM` `ST`

Cytisus × *kewensis* M – broom `ST`

Deutzia corymbosa M `ST`

D. gracilis S `ST`

D. pulchra M `ST`

D. scabra M – beauty bush `ALL` `ST`

Exochorda korolkowii S – pearl bush

Forsythis suspensa 'Nymans' M `ST`

Fuchsia magellanica S `ALL` `ST`

F. m. 'Alba' S `ST`

F. m. 'Hawkshead' S `ST`

Genista aetnensis L `GM`

Hebe albicans 'Autumn Glory' S `ALL` `ST`

H. pinguifolia 'Pagei' S `GM` `ST`

Helianthemum S – rock rose `ALL` `ST`

Hydrangea aspera Villosa Group M

H. paniculata 'Grandiflora' T

Hypericum calycinum S `ALL` `ST`

H. 'Hidcote' S `GM` `ST`

H. moserianum S `GM` `ST`

Kerria japonica 'Pleniflora' M `GM` `ALL` `ST`

Kolkwitzia amabilis 'Pink Cloud' M – beauty bush `ALL` `ST`

Lavatera × *clementii* 'Barnsley' M – tree mallow `ALL` `ST`

L. × *c.* 'Burgundy Wine' `ST`

Magnolia grandiflora T

M. kobus M

M. × *loebneri* 'Leonard Messel' M/T `GM`

Paeonia × *lemoinei* 'Souvenir de Maxine Cornu' S/M – tree peony `ALL`

P. lutea var. 'Ludlowii' M `ST`

P. suffruticosa 'Nigata Akashigata' S/M

Phygelius capensis S Cape figwort `GM` `ALL` `ST`

Piptanthus nepalensis M `ST`

Potentilla fruticosa 'Abbotswood' S `ALL` `ST`

P. f. 'Daydawn' S `ST`

P. f. 'Red Ace' S `ST`

P. f. 'Tilford Cream' S `GM` `ST`

Rubus 'Benenden' T `ALL` `ST`

Spiraea 'Arguta' M

S. japonica 'Anthony Waterer' M `ST`

Tamarix ramosissima 'Pink Cloud' M – tamarisk `ST`

T. tetrandra M `GM` `ST`

Viburnum opulus T `ST`

V. o. 'Sterile' T `ST`

V. plicatum 'Mariesii' M `ALL` `ST`

Weigela florida 'Alexandra' M/S `ALL` `ST`

W. f. 'Pink Poppet' S `ST`

Xantheroceras sorbifolium T `GM` `ST`

Shrubs for Autumn Effect

Berberis thunbergii 'Red Chief' M `GM` `ALL` `ST`

B. trigona 'Orange King' M `ST`

Colutea arborescens T – bladder senna

Cotinus 'Flame' T `ALL` `ST`

Cotoneaster dammeri S `ST`

C. × *watereri* T `GM` `ALL` `ST`

Euonymus alatus M – spindleberry `ALL` `ST`

Leycesteria formosa M – pheasant berry `ST`

Parrotia persica M/T – irontree

Rosa glauca T `GM` `ST`

R. moyesei T `ST`

R. rugosa M/T `ST`

Stranvaesia davidiana T `ST`

Shrubs and Bamboos for Screening

Aucuba japonica 'Crotonifolia' T `ST`

Corylus avellana 'Aurea' M – golden hazel `ST`

Elaeagnus ebbingei 'Gilt Edge' T `GM` `ST`

Fargesia murielae T – bamboo `ST`

Hippophae rhamnoides T – sea buckthorn `GM` `ALL` `ST`

Ilex aquifolium T – holly `GM` `ALL` `ST`

I. a. 'Silver Queen' M – variegated holly

Laurus nobilis T – bay `GM` `ST`

Osmanthus heterophyllus M/T

Phyllostachys aureosulcata 'Spectabilis' T – golden bamboo

Prunus lusitanica T – Portuguese laurel `ST`

Quercus ilex T – holm oak `ST`

Rhamnus alaternus T – buckthorn `ST`

HEDGES

Buxus sempervirens S – box `GM` `ALL` `ST`

B. s. 'Latifolia Maculata' S `ST`

Carpinus betulus T – hornbeam `GM` `ALL` `ST`

Crataegus laevigata T – hawthorn `ALL` `ST`

Cupressocyparis leylandii T – Leyland cypress `GM` `ST`

Escallonia 'Slieve Donard' M `ST`

Fagus sylvatica T – beech `ALL` `ST`

Ilex aquifolium M – holly

Ligustrum ovalifolium 'Aureum' M –
  golden variegated privet ALL ST
L. vulgare T – privet ST
Prunus cerasifera 'Pissardii' T ST
Taxus baccata T – yew GM ST
Thuja plicata T – western red cedar

CLEMATIS

ALL SPECIES AND CULTIVARS ARE LIME-TOLERANT;
ASPECT: S = SOUTH, N = NORTH, E = EAST, W =
WEST, ANY = ANY ASPECT

'Alba Luxurians' ANY GM ST
'Betty Corning' ANY GM ST
'Bill Mackenzie' ANY ST
'Comtesse de Bouchaud' ANY GM
'Ernest Markham' SEW GM ST
'Francis Rivis' SEW GM ST
'Jackmanii' SEW GM
'John Huxtable' ANY GM
'Marie Boisselot' ANY GM
'Marjorie' ANY ST
'Minuet' ANY GM ST
'Mme Julia Correvon' ANY GM ST
'Perle d'Azur' SEW
'Polish Spirit' ANY GM ST
'Prince Charles' ANY GM ST
'Venosa Violacea' ANY GM ST
'Victor Hugo' ANY ST
C. armandii 'Snowdrift' S
C. cirrhosa 'Freckles' S GM ST
C. connata ANY
C. jouiniana 'Praecox' ANY ST
C. macropetala SEW
C. m. var. *rubens* 'Tetrarose' ANY ST
C. montana var. *grandiflora* ANY GM ST
C. rehderiana ANY GM ST
C. serratifolia ANY ST

CLIMBERS AND WALL SHRUBS

ASPECT: S = SOUTH, N = NORTH, E = EAST,
W = WEST, ANY = ANY ASPECT
Pears, apples, cherries, peaches, plums and other
trees and shrubs may be trained against walls

Abutilon × *suntense* 'Jermyns' SW GM ST
Actinidia kolomikta 'Tricolor' SEW GM

Akebia quinata EW ST
Carpenteria californica S GM
Ceanothus S ALL
Celastrus orbiculatus ANY ST
Chaenomeles speciosa 'Moerloosei' ANY GM ALL ST
Cotoneaster horizontalis ANY GM ALL ST
Cytisus battandieri S – Moroccan broom GM
Forsythia suspensa 'Nymans' ANY ALL ST
Fremontodendron 'California Glory' S GM
Garrya elliptica 'James Roof' ANY GM
Hedera helix 'Buttercup' SEW ALL ST
H. h. 'Goldheart' ANY ST
H. h. 'Sagittifolia Variegata' ANY ST
Hydrangea anomala subsp. *petiolaris* ANY GM ST
Jasminum nudiflorum ANY GM ST
J. officinalis S GM
Laburnum × *watereri* 'Vossii' ANY GM ALL ST
Lonicera etrusca ANY – honeysuckle GM ST
L. periclymenum 'Belgica' SEW – early Dutch
  honeysuckle ST
L. p. 'Heaven Scent' SEW ST
L. p. 'Serotina' SEW GM ST
Magnolia grandiflora S
Parthenocissus henryana EWN – Chinese Virginia
  creeper GM
P. quinquefolia ANY – Virginia creeper GM
Passiflora caerula S – blue passion flower GM
P. c. 'Constance Elliot' S – white passion flower
P. c. racemosa S – red passion flower
Phygelius capensis SEW GM
Polygonum baldschuanicum ANY – Russian vine ST
Pyracantha 'Golden Charmer' ANY – firethorn
  ALL ST
P. 'Orange Charmer' ANY ST
P. 'Soleil d'Or' ANY ST
Ribes speciosum ANY GM ST
Schizophragma hydrangeoides SEW
Solanum crispum 'Glasnevin' S GM
S. laxum 'Album' S GM
Stauntonia hexaphylla S ST
Trachelospermum asiaticum S GM
Wisteria floribunda S – Japanese wisteria ALL
W. f. 'Alba' S – white Japanese wisteria GM
W. f. 'Multijuga' S GM
W. sinensis S – wisteria GM
W. s. 'Alba' S – white wisteria GM
W. s. 'Pink Ice' S
W. × *formosa* 'Black Dragon' S

PERENNIAL CLIMBERS

Humulus lupulus 'Aureus' SEW – golden hop GM ST
Lathyrus latifolius S – perennial sweet pea GM ST

ROSES

Rambler Roses

Rosa banksiae, yellow, 6m height ST 'Albéric Barbier', cream, 4m height GM ST
'Albertine', salmon pink, 4m height GM ST
'Bobbie James', white, 4.5m height GM ST
'Climbing Cécile Brunner', pink, 3.5m height GM ST
'Dorothy Perkins', pink, 2.5m height ST
'Ethel', pink, 5m height ST
'François Juranville', pink, 4m height ST
'Kiftsgate', white, 8m height GM ST
'New Dawn', pale pink, 3m height GM
'Paul Transom', salmon pink, 3m height GM
'Phyllis Bide', gold/pink, 2.5m height GM ST
'Rambling Rector', white 5m height GM ST
'Sanders White', white, 3m height GM
'Wedding Day' ST

Climbers and Pillar Roses

'Alchymist', gold, 4m height
'Aloha', pink, 2.5m height GM
'Climbing Étoile d'Hollande', crimson, 3m height GM
'Climbing Iceberg', white, 1.5m height GM ST
'Climbing Lady Hillingdon'
'Climbing Mme Caroline Testout', pink, 4m height GM ST
'Constance Spry' pink, 2m height GM
'Guinée', red, 3m height
'Maigold', gold, 2.5m height ST
'Mme Alfred Carrière', cream, 3.5m height GM
'Parkdirektor Riggers', scarlet, 3.5m height
'Penny Lane', buff cream, 3.5m height GM
'Pink Perpétue' pink, 2.5m height ST
'The Pilgrim' yellow, 2m height ST
'Zéphirine Drouin' pink, 2.5m height

Historic and Hybrid Musk Roses

Rosa gallica officinalis syn 'Apothecary's Rose' red GM ST
R. g. 'Robert le Diable', mauve ST
R. g. 'Rosamunda' syn *R. g.* 'Versicolor', red/white stripes ST
'Rose de Rescht', cerise GM ST 'Buff Beauty', buff GM
'Céleste' syn 'Celestial, pink GM ST
'Comte de Chambord' syn 'Madame Knorr', pink GM ST
'Cornelia', salmon pink GM ST
'Felicia', pink GM ST
'Ferdinand Pichard', red/white stripes GM ST
'Jacques Cartier' syn 'Marchesa Boccella', pink GM
'Königin van Dänemark' syn 'Queen of Denmark', pink GM ST
'Maiden's Blush', pink GM ST
'Mme Pierre Oger', pink
'Mme Plantier', white ST
'Penelope', cream GM ST
'Reine des Violettes', mauve
'White Rose of York' syn *R.* 'Alba Semiplena' ST

Rugosa Roses

Rosa rugosa 'Alba', white GM ST
'Blanche Double de Coubert', white GM ST
'Fimbriata', pale pink ST
'Fru Dagmar Hastrup', pink GM ST
'Martin Frobisher', pink ST
'Mrs Doreen Pike', pink ST
'Pink Grootendorst', pink GM ST
'Roseraie de l'Häye', purple GM ST

Floribunda Roses

'Chinatown', yellow GM
'Frensham', scarlet
'Iceberg', white GM

Modern Shrub Roses

Large
'Cerise Bouquet', cerise GM ST
'Fred Loads', scarlet GM
'Golden Wings', gold GM ST

'Leverkusen', yellow GM ST
'Nevada', cream GM ST

Medium and Small
'Ballerina', pink with white centre GM ST
'Bonica', pink GM ST
'Flower Carpet', cerise ST
'Flower Carpet White', white GM ST
'Marjorie Fair', red with white centre GM ST
'Rose Gaujard', pink
'Smarty', pink ST
'The Fairy', pink GM ST
'Yesterday', purple GM

David Austin's English Roses

'English Garden', buff
'Heritage', pink ST
'Lucetta', pale pink ST
'Mayflower', strong pink ST
'Sharifa Asma', pale peach
'Shropshire Lass', flesh pink ST
'Sweet Juliet', buff yellow ST

Rosa pimpinellifolia – Scottish or Burnet roses

'Dunwich Rose', yellow ST
'Lochinvar', blush pink
'Mary, Queen of Scots', purple and lilac grey ST
'Stanwell Perpetual', blush pink

Species Roses

'Duplex', pink – Wolley Dod's rose
'Geranium' GM ST
Rosa fedtschenkoana, white ST
R. glauca, pink GM ST
R. moyesii
R. × odorata 'Mutabilis', yellow/orange/red (also known as 'changeable Chinaman' or 'butterfly rose')
R. primula – white incense rose GM ST
R. rubiginosa 'Mannings Blush', blush pink ST
R. sericea subsp. *omeiensis* var. *pteracantha*, white ST
R. xanthina 'Canary Bird', yellow GM ST
R. xanthina f. *hugonis*, yellow GM

BULBS, CORMS AND RHIZOMES

Agapathus 'Headbourne Hybrids' ALL ST
Allium caeruleum GM ALL ST
A. carinatum subsp. *pulchellum* GM ST
A. christophii GM ST
A. cowanii ST
A. flavum GM ST
A. hollandicum 'Purple Sensation' GM ST
A. karataviense GM ST
A. moly ST
Anemone blanda GM ST
A. nemorosa GM ST
A. n. 'Robinsoniana' GM ST
Anthericum liliago var. *major* – St Bernard's lily GM ST
Arum italicum 'Marmoratum' GM ST
Camassia cusuckii 'Zwanenburg'
C. leichtlinii ALL ST
C. l. 'Alba Plena' ST
Chionodoxa luciliae – Glory of the Snow GM ALL ST
Commelina tuberosa
Convallaria majalis – lily-of-the-valley ST
C. m. 'Variegata' ST
Crinum powellii GM
C. p. 'Album' GM
Crocosmia 'Lucifer' GM ALL ST
Crocus chrysanthus 'Blue Pearl' GM ALL ST
C. c. 'Cream Beauty' GM ST
C. tommasinianus ST
C. t. 'Barr's Purple' ST
C. vernus 'Pickwick' ST
Cyclamen coum GM ALL ST
C. c. Pewter Group ST
C. hederifolium ST
C. repandum ST
Eranthis hyemalis – winter aconite GM
Erythronium dens-canis 'Pagoda' ST
E. d. 'White Splendour' ST
Eucomis comosa
Fritillaria acmopetala GM ALL ST
F. imperialis – Crown Imperial
F. meleagris – snake's head fritillary
F. pyrenaica GM
Galanthus elwesii – giant snowdrop GM ALL
G. ikariae
G. nivalis – common snowdrop GM ST
G. n. viridapice

G. reginae-olgae
G. 'S. Arnott'
Galtonia candicans GM
Hemerocallis – day lily ST
Hyacinthoides hispanica – Spanish bluebell ST
H. non-scripta – English bluebell ST
Hyacinthus orientalis 'Delft Blue' – hyacinth
Iris ensata GM
I. foetidissima – stinking iris, Gladdon iris GM ST
I. germanica – bearded iris GM ST
I. 'Holden Clough' GM ST
I. pallida 'Argentea Variegata'
I. pseudoacorus – yellow flag GM
I. sibirica 'Silver Edge' GM
I. s. 'Soft Blue' GM
Iris unguicularis GM ST
Leucojum aestivum 'Gravetye Giant' GM
Lilium amabile – lily
L. candidum GM
L. carnioicum
L. 'Golden Splendour' GM
L. henryi GM
L. martagon GM
L. martagon var. *album* GM
L. monadelphum
L. 'Pink Perfection' GM
L. pomponium
L. regale GM
L. × testaceum GM
Muscari armeniacum – grape hyacinth GM ST
M. botryoides 'Album' ST
M. comosum 'Plumosum' ST
M. macrocarpum ST
Narcissus – daffodil
N. 'Carlton' GM
N. 'Cassata'
N. 'February Gold' GM ST
N. 'Golden Harvest'
N. 'Jenny' GM ST
N 'Jetfire' GM
N. 'King Alfred'
N. minimus ST
N. 'Mount Hood' GM
N. poeticus recurvus – poet's narcissus, 'Pheasant Eye' ST
N. pseudonarcissus– Lent lily GM ST
N. 'Spellbinder' GM
N. 'Tête-à-Tête' GM ST

N. 'Thalia'
N. triandrus – angel's tears ST
Nectaroscordum siculum ST
Nerine bowdenii – naked lady GM ST
Ornithogalum nutans GM ST
O. umbellatum – star of Bethlehem ST
Puschinia scilloides var. *libanotica* – striped squill ST
Scilla bifolia – squill GM ALL ST
S. peruviana ST
S. siberica – squill GM ST
Sisyrinchium angustifolium – blue-eyed grass ST
S. striatum ALL ST
Tulipa batalinii 'Bright Gem' – tulip GM
T. humilis 'Persian Pearl' ST
T. praestans 'Fusilier' GM ST
T. sprengeri ST
T. sylvestris
T. turkestanica ST
Zantedeschia aethipioca 'Crowborough' – white arum lily GM

HERBACEOUS PLANTS

Achillea millefolium ALL ST
Anchusa azurea 'Loddon Royalist' ALL ST
Anemone japonica 'Honorine Jobert' GM ST
Aquilegia vulgaris McKana Group – Columbine ALL ST
A. v. 'Norah Barlow' GM ST
Artemesia absinthium 'Lambrook Silver' ALL ST
A. canescens ST
A. ludoviciana 'Silver Queen' ST
Aster amellus 'Sonia' – Michaelmas daisy, Italian starwort
A. a. 'Lac de Genève'
A. a. 'Vanity'
A. sedifolius
Astrantia ST
Baptisia australis GM
Brunnera macrophylla 'Jack Frost' ST
Campanula lactiflora 'Prichard's Variety' ST
C. persicifolia ST
Centaurea – cornflower ALL ST
Centranthus ruber – red valerian ST
C. r. 'Albus' – white valerian ST
Chamerion angusifolium 'Album' – white willowherb ST

C. a. 'Stahl Rose'
Crambe cordifolia ALL
Cynara cardunculus – cardoon GM ST
Dianthus 'Dad's Favourite' – pink ALL ST
Dianthus deltoides – maiden pink GM ST
D. 'Monica Wyatt' GM ST
D. 'Musgrave's Pink' ST
D. 'Paisley Gem' ST
Digitalis ferruginia – rusty foxglove GM ST
D. lanata – woolly foxglove ST
D. lutea – yellow foxglove ST
D. purpurea Sutton's Excelsior hybrids – foxglove ST
Euphorbia characias subsp. *wulfenii* 'Lambrook Gold' GM ALL ST
E. amygdaloides var. *robbiae* ST
E. cyparissias ST
E. griffithii 'Fireglow' ST
E. × *martinii* GM
E. myrsinites GM ST
E. polychroma GM ST
E. rigida ST
Geranium cinereum 'Ballerina' GM ALL ST
G. clarkei 'Kashmir White' GM ST
G. macrorrhizum GM ST
G. oxonianum 'Walter's Gift' ST
G. phaeum – mourning widow ST
G. pratense 'Mrs Kendall Clark' GM ST
G. p. 'Plenum Violaceum' ST
G. psilostemon GM ST
G. × 'Rozanne' ST
Helenium
Helleborus argutifolius GM ALL
H. foetidus – stinking hellebore GM ST
H. orientalis hybrids – Lenten rose ST
H. × *sternii*
Knautia macedonica ST
Lamium – deadnettle
L. galeobdolon 'Hermann's Pride' ALL ST
L. orvala ST
Lunaria annua 'Albavariegata' – honesty ALL ST
Lysimachia clethroides GM ST
Macleaya cordata – plume poppy GM ST
Nigella damascena – love-in-a-mist ST
Ophiopogon planiscapus 'Nigrescens' – lily turf GM ST
Paeonia lactiflora 'Duchesse de Nemours' – peony ALL

P. l. 'Sarah Bernhardt' GM
P. l. 'White Wings'
P. mlokosewitschii ST
Papaver orientale 'Marcus Perry' – oriental poppy ALL ST
P. o. 'Black and White' GM ST
P. o. 'Patty's Plum' ST
P. somniferum 'Album' – opium poppy ST
P. s. 'Black Peony' – opium poppy ST
P. s. 'Pink Chiffon' – opium poppy ST
Phlomis fruticosa – Jerusalem sage ALL ST
Phlox Springpearl hybrids
Platycodon grandiflorus – balloon flower GM ST
Romneya coulteri – tree poppy ST
Rudbeckia fulgida 'Goldsturm' GM
Salvia horminum – annual clary ALL ST
S. nemorosa 'Amethyst' GM ST
S. patens 'Cambridge Blue' GM ST
S. sclarea – clary ST
Sedum spectabile 'Autumn Joy' ALL ST
Sisyrinchium striatum s. angustifolium
Stachys bizantina 'Silver Carpet' – lamb's ear ALL ST
Thalictrum delavayi 'Hewitt's Double' – double goat's rue ST
Verbascum Phoenician hybrids ALL ST
Veronica spicata ALL ST
Vinca major 'Variegata' - variegated periwinkle GM ALL ST

GRASSES AND LOW BAMBOOS

Carex comans
C. oshimensis 'Evergold'
Cortaderia selloana 'Pumila' – pampas grass GM ST
C. fulvida ST
Hakonechloa macra 'Aureola' ST
Miscanthus sinensis
Pennisetum alopecuroides – fountain grass ST
Phalaris arundinacea var. *picta* – gardener's garters ST
Pleioblastus variegatus GM ST
Stipa gigantea – golden oats GM
S. tenuissima GM ST

FERNS

Asplenium ceterach – rusty back `ST`
A. scolopendrium – hart's tongue `GM` `ST`
Dryopteris affinis `GM`
D. erythrosora `GM` `ST`
D. filix-mas – male fern `GM` `ST`
D. f. cristata 'Fred Jackson' – crested male fern `ST`
D. wallichiana `GM`
Polystichum munitum `ST`
P. setiferum Plumosum Group – soft shield fern `ST`

ALPINES

All cultivars and species of the plants below should do well.
Campanula cochlearifolia – fairy thimbles `GM` `ST`
C. portenschlagiana `GM` `ST`
Dianthus – pink `ST`
Draba – nailwort `ST`
Dryas octopetala – mountain avens `GM` `ST`
Erodium guttatum – heron's bill `ST`
Geranium 'Ballerina' `GM` `ST`
Parahebe
Phuopsis stylosa – Caucasian crosswort `ST`
Sedum – stonecrop `ST`
Sempervivum – houseleek `ST`

WILD FLOWERS

All cultivars and species of the plants below should do well.
Achillea millefolium – yarrow `ST`
Anacamptis pyramidalis – pyramid orchid `ST`
Anthyllys velneraria – kidney vetch `ST`
Campanula rotundifolia – harebell `ST`
Centaurum erythraea – centaury `ST`
Cephalanthera damasonium – white helleborine `ST`
Dactylorhiza incarnata – marsh orchid (damp places)
D. maculata – spotted orchid `ST`
Daucus corota – wild carrot `ST`
Geranium sanguineum – bloody cranesbill `ST`
Helianthemum – rock rose `ST`
Knautia arvensis – scabious `ST`
Listera ovata – twayblade `ST`

Lotus corniculatus - bird's-foot-trefoil `ST`
Primula veris – cowslips (dry & damp places) `ST`
Prunella vulgaris – self-heal `ST`
Reseda odorata – wild mignonette `ST`
Sanguisorba minor – salad burnet `ST`

VEGETABLES

Broccoli, sprouts, cauliflower and cabbage, peas, celery and celeriac have no objection to alkalinity, but need enriched soils to produce good crops; the following will give a decent performance on thinner topsoil.
asparagus
asparagus pea
beans, runner
beet
beet Swiss chard (try 'Bright Lights' or 'Lucullus')
broad beans (try 'Aquadulce' or 'The Sutton')
carrot (try 'Lisa' or 'Parmex')
climbing French bean (try 'Blue Lake')
courgette
cucumber, outdoor
French bean (try 'Hestia')
kale
leeks (try 'Musselburgh Improved' or 'Toledo')
lettuce (try 'Lollo Rosso', 'Funly', loose-leaved varieties or 'Little Gem')
mangetout peas
parsnip (try 'Avonresister')
potato (earlies: try 'Pentland Javelin', 'Arran Pilot', 'Foremost' or 'Arran Banner'; maincrop: try 'Pentland Crown', 'Nicola' or 'Pink Fir Apple')
pumpkin
runner beans (try 'Desiree' or 'Hestia')
spinach
spinach beet
squash

PERENNIALS

rhubarb (try 'Hawke's Champagne', 'Timperley Early' or 'Stockbridge Arrow')
root/Jerusalem artichoke (try 'Fuseau')
horseradish

SOFT FRUIT

blackcurrants (try 'Ben Connan' **GM**)
blackberries (try 'Adrienne' or 'Fantasia' **GM**) **ST**
gooseberries (try 'Careless' **GM** , 'Pax' or
    'Whiham's Industry' **GM**) **ST**
grape, indoor ('Black Hamburgh', dessert)
grape, outdoor (try 'Madeleine Sylvaner' or
    'Mueller-Thurgau', dessert/wine) **ST**
raspberry (try 'Malling Jewel' **GM** , 'Glen Magna'
    or 'Terri-Louise') **ST**
strawberry

FRUIT TREES

apple
    'Ashmead's Kernel' **GM** (dessert)
    'Blenheim Orange' **GM** (dessert/cooker)
    'Bramley's Seedling' **GM** (cooker)
    'Crawley Beauty' **ST** (cooker)
    'Egremont Russet' **GM** (dessert) **ST**
    'Fiesta' **GM** (dessert)
    'Greensleeves' **GM** (dessert/cooker)
    'Grenadier' **GM** (cooker)
    'Idared' **GM** (dessert/cooker) **ST**
    'James Grieve' **GM** (dessert)
    'Laxton's Fortune' **GM** (dessert)
    'Lord Lambourne' **GM** (dessert) **ST**
    'Pixie' **GM** (dessert)
    'Sunset' **GM** (dessert)
    'Worcester Pearmain' **GM** (dessert) pear
    'Beth' **GM** (dessert)
    'Concorde' **GM** (dessert)
    'Conference' **GM** (dessert)
    'Doyenne du Comice' **GM** (dessert)
cherry (try 'Celeste' or 'Cherokee')
fig ('Brown Turkey') **GM** **ST**
plum (try 'Victoria' **GM** , 'Jubileum', 'Majorie's
    Seedling' **GM** or 'Oullin's Gage' **GM**) **ST**
quince, *Cydonia oblonga* (try 'Meech's Prolific')
    ST
medlar, *Mespilus germanica* **ST**
cobnuts and filberts (try 'Cosford', 'Kentish Cob'
    or 'Red Filbert') **ST**

HERBS

Allium schoenoprasum – chive **ST**
Anethum graveolens – dill **ST**
Angelica archangelica – angelica
Anthriscus cerefolium – chervil **ST**
Artemesia dracunculus – French tarragon **ST**
Foeniculum vulgare – fennel **ST**
Hyssopus officinalis – hyssop **ST**
Lavandula angustifolia – English lavender **ST**
Levisticum officinale – lovage **ST**
Melissa officinalis 'Aurea' – variegated lemon balm
    ST
Mentha piperata – peppermint
M. p. 'Citrata' – eau de Cologne mint
M. pulegia 'Cunningham' – creeping pennyroyal
M. suaveolens – apple mint
M. s. graveolens – pineapple mint
M. × *villosa* var. *alopecuroides* – Bowles apple mint
Myrrhis odorata – sweet ciceley
Oregano vulgare – marjoram, oregano **ST**
O. vulgare 'Curly Gold' – golden marjoram **GM** **ST**
Petroselinum crispum – parsley
Rosmarinus officinalis – rosemary **ST**
Salvia officinalis – sage **ST**
S. o. 'Berggarten' – sage **ST**
S. o. 'Icterina' – variegated sage **GM** **ST**
S. o. purpurascens – purple sage **GM** **ST**
Satureja hortensis – summer savory **ST**
S. montana – winter savory **ST**
Thymus × *citriodorus* – lemon-scented thyme **ST**
T. serpyllum – creeping thyme **ST**
T. s. 'Minor' **ST**
T. vulgaris – common thyme **ST**
Valeriana officinalis – valerian

Plants Unlikely to Succeed on Alkaline Soils

TREES

Abies – except *A. cephalonica,
A. pinsapo* and *A.* × *vilmorinii*
Castanea
Cercidiphyllum
Embothrium
Exochorda – except *E. korolkowii*
Liquidambar
Nothofagus
Nyssa
Pinus – 5-needled species
Quercus rubra and other oaks
grown for autumn colour

SHRUBS

Arctostaphylos
Calluna
Camellia
Clethra
Cornus florida
Corylopsis – although *C. pauciflora*
may succeed in a good depth of
soil
Crinodendron
Cytisus multiflorus, C. scoparius –
although may succeed in a
good depth of soil
Daboecia
Desfontainea
Enkianthus

Erica (except *E. carnea, E.
mediterranea, E. darleyensis,
E. terminalis*, but even these
need a good depth of soil)
Escallonia virgata
Eucryphia
Exocorda racemosa
Fabiana
Fothergilla
Gaultheria
Hamamelis
Hydrangea sargentiana
Kalmia
Leptospermum
Leucothoe fontanesiana
Lomatis ferruginea
Magnolia (except *M. grandiflora,
M. kobus, M.* × *loebneri,
M. wilsonii* and *M. sieboldii*)
Menziesia
Pachysandra
Pernettya
Pieris
Rhododendron (although the
recently introduced 'Inkarho'
rhododendrons on lime-tolerant
rootstock will take a pH of 7.0
and slightly above)
Skimmia
Spiraea billiardi, douglasii, japonia
Tsuga (except *T. canadensis* and
even this needs depth of soil)
Vaccinium

HERBACEOUS PLANTS

Cornus canadensis
Gentiana
Lithodora
Lupinus – although it may survive
in a good depth of soil
Meconopsis betonicifolia (blue
Himalayan poppy)

FERNS

Genera such as *Blechnum,
Cryptogramma, Osmunda* and
Thelypteris

BULBS, CORMS AND TUBERS

Cardiocrinum giganteum
Iris kaempferi, I. douglasiana and
I. innominata
*Lilium auratum, L. japonicum,
L. lancifolium, L. leichtlinii,
L. medeoloides, L. neigherrense,
L. nepalense, L. rubellum,
L. speciosum, L. wallichianum*
and oriental hybrids
Narcissus bulbocodium
Nomocharis

FRUIT

blueberry
cranberry

Gardens on Alkaline Soil

Gardens on chalk tend to be more alkaline than those on limestone, and their owners more aware of the restrictions of growing plants in a high pH soil. Virtually all the opening times of the gardens below are given in one or other or both *The Good Gardens Guide* and *Gardens of England and Wales Open for Charity*, both published annually and either – ideally both – essential accompaniments for the garden visitor. Not all, like Blewbury village, open their gardens every year, and a change of ownership often means that a garden slips from the list.

Beth Chatto's Essex nursery and garden, not mentioned below because it is not on alkaline soil, has many drought-tolerant plants happy on dry soil with a high pH.

BEDFORDSHIRE

VALLEY FORGE – 213 Castle Hill Road, Totternhoe
Half an acre of garden terraced on chalk with pergolas, shrubs, perennials and trees, including the rare Aylesbury prune.

BERKSHIRE

WELFORD PARK – near Newbury
Fine trees and recently restored gardens in spacious grounds and park (dpuxley@btopenworld.com).

BUCKINGHAMSHIRE

MANOR HOUSE – Bledow
Paved garden, parterres, shrub borders, old roses and walled kitchen garden as well as a water garden fed by chalk springs and 2 acres with sculptures and landscaped planting.
WADDESDON MANOR – near Aylesbury
Victorian, three-dimensional bedding displays, carpet bedding, terraces, fountains, water garden and trees; soil varies from pH 7.5 to 7.8 (www.waddesdon.org.uk).

CAMBRIDGESHIRE

CAMBRIDGE UNIVERSITY BOTANIC GARDEN – Cambridge
Fine trees with limes, chestnuts, willows and conifers predominating, as well as winter garden, limestone rock garden, and much more on alkaline river gravel over chalky marl, pH 7.5 to 7.8 (www.botanic.cam.ac.uk).
CROSSING HOUSE – Shepreth
Cottage garden on chalk beside the railway line with bulbs, shrubs, roses and many unusual plants, including a cut-leaved walnut.
DOCWRA'S MANOR – Shepreth
Romantic, 2½-acre garden divided into compartments by buildings, walls and hedges, with many choice plants, including roses, spurges, clematis, eryngiums and philadelphus.
MILL HOUSE – North End, Bassingbourn
Walls and pergolas on several levels, with many good plants including clematis (millhouseval@btinternet.com).

OPPOSITE PAGE:
Picea glauca *var* albertiana *'Conica', this dwarf spruce grows in a conical shape without pruning.*

CUMBRIA

Levens Hall – near Kendal
Topiary garden designed in 1694 and retaining its original trees and plan, additionally, the earliest English ha-ha, herb garden, spring and summer bedding and more; on limestone, with neutral to slightly alkaline soil (www.levenshall.com).

DORSET

Cranborne Manor – Cranborne
Beautiful historic garden on chalk laid out in the seventeenth century and enlarged in the twentieth; walls and yew hedges, apple tunnel, herb and mount gardens, white garden and much more. (www.cranborne.co.uk).

Kingston Maurward – near Dorchester
35 acres of gravel varying from a few centimetres to a metre and more over chalk; terraces and gardens divided by hedges and balustrades hold many unusual plants including National Collections of penstemons and salvias; tree trail and 5-acre lake (www.kmc.ac.uk).

GLOUCESTERSHIRE

Hidcote Manor – near Chipping Campden
Famous garden with a series of outdoor 'rooms' with many rare trees and shrubs, and outstanding herbaceous borders; untreated soil measures around pH 8.0, but about 6.5 where Lawrence Johnston imported soil in the 1930s for acid lovers (www.nationaltrust.org.uk).

Highgrove House – near Tetbury
The Prince of Wales's organic garden with thyme walk, topiary, wild flower meadow, stumpery and water features is not open to the public, but organized groups may apply for an invitation at: The Prince of Wales Office, St James's Palace, London SW1 1AA (the waiting list is currently about four years' long).

Kiftsgate Court – near Chipping Campden
Stunning views and many trees, climbers and shrubs, including tree peonies, hydrangeas, abutilons, species and old-fashioned roses, including the giant rose 'Kiftsgate'; pockets of highly alkaline soil but otherwise neutral (www.kiftsgate.co.uk).

Rodmarton Manor – near Cirencester
Fine 'Arts and Crafts' house facing 8 acres with winter garden, troughery, topiary, wild garden, kitchen garden and magnificent herbaceous borders (www.rodmarton-manor.co.uk).

Trull House – near Tetbury
Formal and informal areas, including lily pond, herbaceous borders, wilderness, spring bulbs and mature trees (simonmitchell@btconnect.com).

Westbury Court – near Westbury-on-Severn
Formal seventeenth-century, Dutch-style water garden with canals and summer house. Over 100 plant species as well as vegetables grown before 1700; soil pH varies from 7.3 to 8.0. (www.nationaltrust.org.uk).

HAMPSHIRE

Abbey Cottage – Itchen Abbas
Organic garden on chalk linked by steps, slopes and yew corridor; many excellent plants including species clematis, *Cornus alternifolia* 'Argentea' and ancient, well-groomed apple trees.

Bramdean House – Bramdean
On chalk; trees, shrubs, bulbs, fine kitchen garden with vegetables and sweet peas; most outstanding are the mirrored herbaceous borders, rivers of colour through the summer months.

Brandy Mount House – Alresford
Plantsman's 1-acre garden with spring bulbs, pulmonarias, epimediums, trilliums, hellebores and geraniums; National Collections of snowdrops and daphnes.

Fairfield House – Hambledon
Mature cedars, limes, copper beeches and other trees on chalk, with a fine collection of old-fashioned and species roses planted informally over 5 acres.

Farleigh House – near Basingstoke
Exemplary modern garden on chalk in classic tradition with kitchen garden, topiary, fountain garden with perennials, simple maze, Scots pines and lake.

HINTON AMPNER – Hinton Ampner
Terraced gardens on chalk, with immaculate hedging and topiary and splendid views; plants include *Philadelphus*, *Cotinus*, salvias, roses and *Agapanthus*; there is an adjacent acid clay strip for calcifuges (www.nationaltrust.org.uk).

LITTLE COURT – Crawley
Walled country garden with bulbs, climbers and perennials, and traditional kitchen garden (elkslc@onetel.net.uk).

WHITE WINDOWS – Longparish
Three small and immaculate connecting gardens belonging to the former chairman of the Hardy Plant Society and containing many unusual plants including *Ptelea trifoliata* 'Aurea' and *Malus transitoria* with hawthorn-like leaves.

HERTFORDSHIRE

BENINGTON LORDSHIP – near Stevenage
Hill-top garden on castle ruins overlooking lakes, with bulbs, rose garden, borders, ornamental kitchen garden and flights of steps everywhere (www.beningtonlordship.co.uk).

KNEBWORTH HOUSE – Knebworth
Gardens laid out by Lutyens in 1910, with pollarded lime avenues, restored maze, herb garden, herbaceous borders, formal gardens, woodland and more; clay over chalk, pH 8.5 and over in places (www.knebworthhouse.com).

ISLE OF WIGHT

BADMINTON – Clatterford Shute
Mixed borders planted for all-year interest, good views and natural chalk stream.

KENT

GOODNESTONE PARK – Wingham
About 10 acres on chalk with trees, bulbs, walled garden and old roses, new gravel garden, salvias and good perennials; also an acre of woodland in acid pocket for rhododendrons and other calcifuges (www.goodnestoneparkgardens.co.uk).

ROCK FARM – Nettlestead
Plantsman's collection of shrubs, trees and perennials for alkaline soil; extensive herbaceous border, vegetable area, bog garden and plantings around two large natural ponds (www.rockfarmhousebandb.co.uk).

THORNTON FRIARS – Thurnham
2 acres of chalk by the Pilgrim's Way, with unusual shrubs and trees; lawns and 12-acre park.

LINCOLNSHIRE

GUNBY HALL – Spilsby
7 acres of formal and walled gardens with herb garden, old roses, herbaceous border, trees and shrubs beside house built in 1700; clay over chalk; pH varies considerably (gunbyhall@ic24.net).

NORFOLK

THE PLANTATION GARDEN – Norwich
Restored Victorian garden in old chalk and flint quarry, with Italianate terrace, Gothic fountain, rustic bridge and summerhouse, surrounded by mature trees (www.plantationgarden.co.uk).

OXFORDSHIRE

BLEWBURY VILLAGE – near Didcot
Many good gardens in this village on the chalk spring line, including Hall Barn with herbaceous borders, thatched cob wall and clear stream.

LANGFORD VILLAGE – near Lechlade
Some beautiful gardens open annually in this limestone village, including School House, a formal courtyard garden with summerhouse and old roses formerly owned by Sir Hardy Amies, and Lime Tree Cottage, with roses and herbaceous border.

OXFORD UNIVERSITY BOTANIC GARDEN – Oxford
The oldest botanic garden in Britain, founded in 1621 for physicians' herbal requirements, with representatives of 90 per cent of the families of flowering plants; a National Collection of *Euphorbia*;

surrounded by a Grade 1 listed wall and entered through a fine archway (botanic-garden.ox.ac.uk).
STANSFIELD – 49 High Street,
Stanford-in-the-Vale
Plantsman's garden on alkaline soil with many uncommon plants shown in appropriate scree, damp, shade or woodland conditions.

SOMERSET

BOTANIC NURSERY – near Atworth
Open Fridays and Saturdays 10.00 to 17.00. Small display garden attached to nursery specializing in a wide variety of lime-tolerant plants (www.thebotanicnursery.com).
CITY OF BATH BOTANICAL GARDENS –
Royal Victoria Park
Formed in 1887, this is one of the finest collections of trees, shrubs and herbaceous plants on limestone in the West Country.
HADSPEN – near Wincanton
Superb 5-acre garden on alkaline clay with water garden, roses, vegetables, and famed for its curved walled colour border, its borders of gold and silver, and beech tunnel with hellebores and later hostas (hadspengarden.co.uk).

SURREY

LONG BARTON – 12 Longdown Road, Guildford
This garden on shallow chalk has fine views, as well as varied shrubs, including a collection of Japanese maples and tree peonies.
POLESDEN LACEY – near Dorking
30 acres on chalk with splendid views of the North Downs; walled gardens and herbaceous border, as well as trees and shrubs, including viburnums, *Cotinus* and *Hydrangea aspersa*; an acid cap near the car park supports rhododendrons and sweet chestnuts (www.nationaltrust.org.uk).

SUSSEX

HIGHDOWN – near Worthing
Originally a chalkpit, this is the garden of Sir Frederick Sterne, who wrote the classic *A Chalk Garden*; a wide variety of bulbs, shrubs and trees is maintained.
MOUNT HARRY HOUSE – Offham
1-acre, terraced garden on chalk, with herbaceous and shrub borders, wild flower walk, laburnum walks, walled garden and dell garden in downland setting.
SHERBURNE HOUSE – Eartham, near Chichester
Garden of 2 acres on chalk with lime-tolerant shrubs, grey-leaved and foliage plants, shrub and climbing roses, potager and wild flower meadow.

WILTSHIRE

CHISENBURY PRIORY – East Chisenbury
Beautiful, 5-acre, mature garden on chalk with herbaceous borders, shrubs, roses and many unusual plants surrounding Queen Anne house.

YORKSHIRE

THE OLD RECTORY – Nunburnholme
Large, informal garden for chalk-loving plants with stream running through; shrubs and herbaceous beds blend into the surrounding countryside.
PARCEVALL HALL – Skyreholme
Geological drama; beds of acid lovers (camellias, *Desfontainea*) over millstone grit sit adjacent to a natural limestone pavement planted with alpines including pinks and daphnes (www.parcevallhallgardens.co.uk).

Bibliography

BOOKS

Baker, Harry (ed.), *The Fruit Garden Displayed* (Cassell, 1991)

Berrisford, Judith M., *Gardening on Lime* (Faber & Faber, 1963)

Bertram Anderson, E., *Gardening on Chalk and Limestone* (Collingridge Ltd, 1965)

Clifton-Taylor, Alec, *The Pattern of English Building* (Faber & Faber, 1987)

Davis, Brian, *The Gardener's Illustrated Encyclopedia of Climbers and Wall Shrubs* (Viking, 1990)

Davis, Brian, *The Gardener's Illustrated Encyclopedia of Trees and Shrubs* (Viking, 1987)

Dyson, Ronald, *Gardening on Chalk and Lime* (Dent & Sons Ltd, 1977)

Evison, J.R.B., *Gardening on Lime and Chalk* (Wisley Handbook, 1985)

Hessayon, Dr D.G., *The Vegetable Expert* (Expert Books, 1995)

Hilliers' Manual of Trees and Shrubs (Hillier & Sons, 1973)

Jefferson-Brown, Michael and Howland, Harris, *The Gardener's Guide to Growing Lilies* (David and Charles, 1995)

Larkcom, Joy (ed.), *The Vegetable Garden Displayed* (Batsford, 1994)

Muir, Ken, *Grow Your Own Fruit* (Ken Muir, 1999)

Quest-Ritson, Charles and Brigid, *Royal Horticultural Society Encyclopedia of Roses* (Dorling Kindersley, 2003)

Royal Horticultural Society Plant Finder (Dorling Kindersley, 2004)

Stern, F.C., *A Chalk Garden* (Nelson & Sons Ltd, 1960)

Trueman, A.E., *Geology and Scenery in England and Wales* (Pelican, 1971)

CATALOGUES

Allwood Bros
Summerfield Nursery, London Road,
Hassocks, W. Sussex
BN6 9NB
www.allwoodbros.co.uk
Pink and carnation specialist.

Botanic Nursery
Rookery Nursery, Cottles Lane,
Atworth, Melksham
Wiltshire
SN12 8HU
www.thebotanicnursery.com
Specializing in lime-tolerant trees, shrubs and herbaceous plants.

Coombland Nursery
Coneyhurst, Billinghurst
West Sussex
RH14 9DY
www.coombland.co.uk
Hardy geranium specialist.

David Austin Roses
Bowling Green Lane, Albrighton
Wolverhampton
WV7 3HB
www.davidaustinroses.com

Grafted Walnut Trees
The Manse, Capel Isaac
Llandeilo, Carmarthenshire
Wales
SA19 7TN
www.graftedwalnuts.co.uk
Walnut specialist.

Old Court Nurseries
Walwyn Road, Colwall
Malvern
WR13 6QE
www.autumnasters.co.uk
Wide selection of Michaelmas daisies, including mildew-free varieties.

Peter Beales Roses
London Road, Attleborough
Norfolk
NR17 1AY
www.classicroses.co.uk

Peter Nyssen Ltd
124 Flixton Road, Urmston
Manchester
M41 5BG
www.peternyssenltd.co.uk
For buying bulbs in bulk.

Thompson & Morgan
Poplar Lane, Ipswich
Suffolk
IP8 3BU
www.thompson-morgan.com
Seedsmen for flowers and vegetables.

Index